The Mysterious & Unknown

Witches

by Peggy J. Parks

ReferencePoint Press™

San Diego, CA

ReferencePoint Press™

For more information, contact
ReferencePoint Press, Inc.
PO Box 27779
San Diego, CA 92198
www.ReferencePointPress.com

Picture credits:
AP/Wide World Photos, 8, 53, 54, 56
Dover Publication, 6, 21, 27
Dreamstime, 78, 80, 82, 83
Fortean Picture Library, 59
Landov, 63
North Wind, 19, 35, 47, 51
Photos.com, 23
Science, Industry & Business Library/New York Public Library/SPL, 38
SPL, 29
Wikipedia, 11, 12, 13

Series design and book layout:
Amy Stirnkorb

LIBRARY OF CONGRESS CATALOGING-IN-PUBLICATION DATA

Parks, Peggy J., 1951-
Witches / by Peggy J. Parks.
p. cm. -- (The mysterious & unknown)
Includes bibliographical references and index.
ISBN-13: 978-1-60152-031-9 (hardback)
ISBN-10: 1-60152-031-X (hardback)
1. Witchcraft--Juvenile literature. 2. Witches--Juvenile literature. I. Title.
BF1566.P28 2008
133.4'3--dc22

2007019093

Contents

FOREWORD

"Strange is our situation here upon earth."
—Albert Einstein

Since the beginning of recorded history, people have been perplexed, fascinated, and even terrified by events that defy explanation. While science has demystified many of these events, such as volcanic eruptions and lunar eclipses, some continue to remain outside the scope of the provable. Do UFOs exist? Are people abducted by aliens? Can some people see into the future? These questions and many more continue to puzzle, intrigue, and confound despite the enormous advances of modern science and technology.

It is these questions, phenomena, and oddities that ReferencePoint Press's *The Mysterious & Unknown* series is committed to exploring. Each volume examines historical and anecdotal evidence as well as the most recent theories surrounding the topic in debate. Fascinating primary source quotes from scientists, experts, and eyewitnesses, as well as in-depth sidebars further inform the text. Full-color illustrations and photos add to each book's visual appeal. Finally, source notes, a bibliography, and a thorough index provide further reference and research support. Whether for research or the curious reader, *The Mysterious & Unknown* series is certain to satisfy those fascinated by the unexplained.

Introduction

The Great Unknown

In the year 1600 six people from Dettingen, Germany, were brutally tortured and executed for the crime of witchcraft. The group, or coven, was composed of Anna and Paul Gamperle, their two adult sons, and two other men, all of whom considered themselves to be witches. Because they knew that witchcraft was illegal, they gathered secretly to celebrate their rites in a cave outside of town. But on July 23, 1600, in the middle of a fierce thunderstorm, they were arrested and taken to officials for questioning. In addition to witchcraft, they were blamed for numerous crimes—including robbery, arson, theft, and nearly 500 deaths—and they were sentenced to die.

In front of a cheering crowd, Anna Gamperle was tied to a stake between her two sons. First an executioner cut off both of her breasts, and as she hung there, helpless and bleeding, he beat her with a metal whip. For the last part of her torture, she was tied to a wheel and was stretched until her arms broke. As the executioner prepared to place her in a spiked metal chair to be burned alive, she died, and her body was thrown into the fire. Her husband and sons, as well as the other two men, were also viciously beaten, and they too were stretched until their arms were broken. But unlike

In Germany and other parts of Europe from the 1400s through the mid-1700s, suspected witches were tortured and burned at the stake. Witches were viewed as evil and had to be burned to dispel this evil.

Anna, they were not fortunate enough to die on the wheel; instead, they were all burned alive at the stake.

The Power of Religion

At the time of such executions in Germany and some other parts of Europe, witches were viewed as wicked creatures who had made pacts with the devil. By allegedly promising their souls to Satan, they were given powers that allowed them to practice evil acts of magic and to torment innocent people. Seldom was there any evidence of witchcraft, but people's fear of what witches were capable of doing was enough to fan the flames of hysteria. Based on trial records, most historians say that from the 1400s through the mid-1700s, somewhere between 40,000 and 100,000 people were executed for witchcraft in Europe.

But witches had not always been perceived in a negative way. In ancient times people who had the ability to heal the sick, make crops grow, or make rain fall were revered almost as though they were gods or goddesses. They were called *wicca* (men) or *wicce* (women), meaning "wise ones," and those terms later came to mean "male witch" (or "wizard") and "female witch." This positive perception of witches took a radical turn during the latter part of the Middle Ages, when Christianity became the dominant religion in Europe. No longer were witches viewed as healers, miracle workers, or people who possessed powers to do good deeds. Instead, anyone suspected of being a witch was held responsible for all bad things that happened, from sickness and disease to storms and droughts. Witchcraft researcher and author Leo Ruickbie writes:

> We have all suffered misfortune of one kind or another from time to time, but did you blame a witch for the problem? Did you accuse a neighbor of casting evil magic? Did you call for her to be hanged or burnt because of it? We all ponder the question of God from time to time, but have you ever sacrificed a black lamb at a crossroads to the Goddess of Witchcraft? Have you ever signed a pact with the Devil and danced at his Sabbath? All of this and more has happened, or been alleged to have happened, in the name of witchcraft.[1]

***Perceptions of witches have varied through the ages from wicked, old hags flying on broom sticks to beautiful, good witches such as Glinda the Good Witch from* The Wizard of Oz.**

Creatures of Mystery

The vast difference between the healers of ancient times and the supposed evildoers of the Middle Ages is indicative of how differently witches have been viewed throughout history. Their perception has ranged from the ugly, wicked crones of children's fairy tales to beautiful, good witches like Glinda in *The Wizard of Oz* or Samantha in the television show *Bewitched.* Today thousands of people claim to be witches. Many of them practice Wicca, which is an earth-based religion that is centered in nature and the seasons. Other self-proclaimed witches do not belong to any religion at all and worship no deities. And while witches no longer have to fear being burned alive or hanged, they often pursue their craft in secret because many people still see witchcraft as dark and evil. An even greater number of people refuse to believe that witchcraft exists, thinking it is nothing more than myth or hocus-pocus. Author and psychic researcher Graham Wyley explains, "If the average person were asked to describe a witch, they would probably tell you that witches do not exist. Witches, they will say, are [imaginary], unkempt old women with black conical hats, warts on their noses, bad teeth and broomsticks, who are believed to create evil spells. The description has become curiously detailed, for a character who doesn't exist."[2]

From the horrors of the witch hunts and mass executions of the past to the witchcraft that is practiced in modern times, witches have long been shrouded in mystery. Whether people believe that they are evil, harmless, or do not exist, they are every bit as mysterious today as they were hundreds of years ago.

Did You Know?

Most historians say that from the 1400s through the mid-1700s, somewhere between 40,000 and 100,00 people were executed for witchcraft in Europe.

CHAPTER 1

The History of Witchcraft

There is no clear, traceable path from the witchcraft of ancient times to the witchcraft of today. Throughout history different cultures have had their own ideas about good and evil, magic, and whether certain people possessed supernatural powers. Yet many historians believe that the practice of witchcraft in one form or another has existed since humans have been on Earth.

The roots of witchcraft can be traced back to the numerous gods and goddesses that people worshipped long ago. These deities represented the people's reverence for the immense power of nature. Ancient peoples were aware that what the earth provided gave them life, and they chose their gods accordingly, as author and self-proclaimed witch Raymond Buckland writes: "Nature was overwhelming. Out of awe and respect for the gusting wind, the violent lightning, the rushing stream, [humans] ascribed to

The roots of witchcraft can be traced back to the gods of nature that people worshipped long ago. Pictured is a sculpture of Neptune, the Greek god of the seas, horses, and earthquakes.

each a spirit, made each a deity . . . a god. This is what we call *animism.* A god controlled that wind. A god controlled the sky. A god controlled the waters. But most of all, a god controlled the all-important hunt . . . a God of Hunting."[3]

The God and Goddess

The reason the hunting god was so revered is because hunting was the very essence of ancient peoples' ability to survive.

Ancient peoples revered goddesses as well as gods. Known as the Venus figures, hundreds of female statues have been discovered across Europe. Pictured is the famous Venus of Willendorf, which was discovered in 1908 and is estimated to be more than 20,000 years old.

Animals provided them with food to eat, skins that could be used for clothing and shelter, and bones that could be crafted into tools and weapons. And since most of the animals that were hunted had horns, people naturally assumed the god of hunting also had horns. They aptly named him the horned god and worshipped him as the deity who presided over the woodlands, the animals, and the hunt. He was also viewed as a symbol of male fertility, energy, and power.

As important and revered as the horned god was, he did not rule alone. He shared his reign over the land with a female deity known by some cultures as the mother goddess. In the same way that people depended on the horned god for their livelihood, they depended on the goddess for the fertility of women so they could bear children. This was especially crucial during ancient times because illness and disease were common and people's life expectancies were short, as Buckland explains: "If the tribe was to continue then there had to be fertility of humans."[4] With the development of agriculture, the goddess became even more important because it was she who blessed the land and kept it fertile so that crops would grow. Historians have learned about people's reverence for goddesses from ancient artifacts. More than 100 statues carved out of stone, bone, or ivory have been discovered over a wide geographical area in Europe. Known as Venus figures, the nude subjects lack any facial features but have exaggerated feminine attributes such as enormous breasts and large buttocks, and some have swollen bellies as though to indicate pregnancy. One of the most famous of these figures is the Venus of Willendorf, which was discovered by archaeologists in 1908 near the town of Willendorf, Austria. The statuette stands just 4-3/8 inches (11 .1cm) high and is estimated to be more than 20,000 years old. Historians do not always agree about what the Venus figures were meant to represent, but many of them are convinced that the artifacts prove that prehistoric peoples worshipped goddesses as well as gods.

Did You Know?

An ancient gravesite of a sorceress was discovered in the area that is now Germany, and archaeologists believe it dates back to the Bronze Age, from 2000 to 5000 B.C. Buried with the sorceress's remains was an unusual collection of items, including the bones of a weasel.

The Wise Ones

To honor their gods and goddesses, people of many cultures held elaborate celebrations. There were rituals and festivals to celebrate fertility and childbirth, successful hunts, and plentiful growing seasons, and esteemed tribal leaders presided over the events. These were the priests and priestesses, who were revered nearly as much as the gods and goddesses they represented. But the exalted leaders' responsibilities went far beyond playing prominent roles at celebrations. By being able to harness the power of the gods, they were thought to possess great wisdom and supernatural powers, and they were consulted about all matters of importance. These sorcerers, as they were often called, were common in many tribes throughout Europe. An ancient gravesite of a sorceress was discovered in the area that is now Germany, and archaeologists believe it dates back to the Bronze Age, from 2000 to 5000 B.C. Buried with the sorceress's remains was an unusual collection of items, including the bones of a weasel, the claw joint of a lynx, snake spinal cords, horse teeth, a broken knife blade, a twig from a tree, and some pieces of fool's gold. Historians can only guess what magical properties the items were thought to possess and how the sorceress may have used them to perform her tasks.

Did You Know?

Shamans were believed to have supernatural powers.

One power that sorcerers reportedly possessed was divination, or the ability to foretell the future. Sorcerers accomplished this feat by using information obtained from omens, dreams, or visions or by reading signs in nature. Author Rosemary Ellen Guiley explains:

> Historically, methods of divination involve either interpretation of natural patterns in the environment or patterns that are formed by the tossing of objects such as sticks, stones or bones. Information is obtained from the way smoke curls from a fire, the shape of an animal bone, the formation of clouds and the markings on organs and entrails of sacrificed animals. . . . Popular in the Middle Ages was the tossing of grain, sand or peas onto the earth to see what could be read from the patterns.[5]

Like sorcerers, shamans were also believed to have supernatural powers. They were spiritual leaders who were highly respected for their great wisdom as well as for their ability to heal people who were sick. They were also revered because they could communicate with, or channel, the spirits of the dead. By tapping into the wisdom of the underworld, shamans were able to increase their knowledge and become even more valuable to the people they served. Journalist and author Margot Adler explains, "Shamanism is best defined as a method to open a door and enter a different reality. A shaman is someone who enters an altered state of consciousness and goes on a journey in order to gather knowledge from a different reality populated by spirit, the spirit of plants and animals, and the divine self both within and around the individual."[6] Before using their powers, shamans put themselves into trances or coaxed their bodies into an altered state of consciousness by smoking herbs, chanting and singing, going without food or sleep, or eating psychoactive (mind-altering) plants. Celtic shamans were known as druids, meaning "knowing the oak." They were the keepers of the sacred oak groves, and they harvested and used the mistletoe that grew around the trees, which was thought to have miraculous healing properties.

Because the Celts were secretive, little is known about them. Yet historians believe that they held the druids in the highest possible esteem. These Celtic priests had many different responsibilities for their tribes, as Ruickbie describes:

> They read omens and conducted sacrifices in the proper manner; they kept the calendar and knew astronomy; and they were learned in herbal medicine and poetry—doctors, poets, priests and astronomers all in one. . . . They would foretell the future by observing hares or the flight of crows and eagles, or by watching the death throes of sacrificial victims and examining their entrails. During religious festivals they would interpret dreams.[7]

The Advent of Christianity

Even though the Celts and other European peoples had worshipped their own gods and goddesses for thousands of years, their beliefs began to be challenged during the early Middle Ages. In the fourth century A.D. the powerful emperor of Rome, Constantine the Great, accepted the Christian faith. Christianity is a monotheistic religion, meaning that adherents recognize only one deity or god. This was, of course, a foreign concept to the people who had revered numerous gods and goddesses since the beginning of time. Armed with his conviction that Christianity should be the dominant religion, Constantine and his followers vowed to stamp out paganism—a word that took on a highly derogatory meaning even though it translates as "people who live in the country." Buckland writes:

> It is only natural to want to get rid of a rival and the Church pulled no punches to do just that. It has frequently been said that the gods of an old religion became the devils of a new. This was certainly the case here. The God of the Old Religion was a horned god. So, apparently, was the Christian's Devil. Obviously then, reasoned the Church, the Pagans were Devil worshippers! . . . Missionaries were particularly prone to label all primitive tribes upon whom they stumbled as devil-worshippers, just because the tribe worshipped a god or gods other than the Christian one.[8]

Did You Know?

Christianity is a monotheistic religion, meaning that adherents recognize only one deity or god. In the fourth century, the first Christian Roman emperor, Constantine, vowed to eliminate paganism, the idolization of many gods.

In the early Middle Ages, people who were thought to be witches or sorcerers and to possess supernatural powers were punished or even sentenced to death. Their alleged crime, however, was not witchcraft; instead, it was heresy, or the act of going against the teachings of Christianity. At that time, most religious leaders scoffed at the idea that anyone could possess supernatural powers, and they did not recognize the existence of witches or witchcraft. Some declared that believing in witches was unchristian and therefore against the law, as history professor Brian A. Pavlac explains:

> The predominant Christian view of witchcraft was that it was an illusion. People might think they were witches, but they were fooling themselves, or the Devil was fooling them. Most authorities thought that witchcraft could do no serious harm, because it was not real. It took the arguments of theologians, a number of inquisitor's manuals, and a series of papal bulls (written letters of judgment and command) to contradict that traditional Christian idea, and identify witchcraft with a dangerous heresy.[9]

The church's rejection of the existence of witchcraft was made public in a papal bull called *Canon Episcopi*, which was introduced in the early tenth century and was believed to be written by an anonymous priest. The canon declared that so-called witches and sorcerers did not possess any of the powers that they had been credited for, and it refuted the popular belief that witches flew in the night accompanied by spirits. It further stated that these people's actual sin was in believing that they had such powers, and it declared that anyone who persisted in believing in witchcraft was guilty of heresy. Even though the document defined witchcraft as a form of devil worship, it declared that such practices were not a threat because they were nothing but foolish delusions. It further stated that because so many people had these mistaken beliefs, that was clearly a sign that their thoughts were being influenced by the devil.

Did You Know?

Thomas Aquinas, the revered medieval theologian and Catholic priest, strongly disagreed that witchcraft was an illusion and was convinced that witches had powers that were given to them by the devil.

Clamping Down

The *Canon Episcopi* was considered an important document, and its declarations were embraced by many Christian leaders. Yet numerous others refused to be swayed from their belief that witchcraft did indeed exist. As Christianity continued to grow more powerful and influential throughout Europe, increasing numbers of church leaders began to challenge the canon. Many of these leaders publicly stated that not only did witchcraft exist, but it was also an evil and dangerous threat to humankind. Church officials issued a series of papal bulls against the canon. One of the most influential of these leaders was a theologian named Thomas Aquinas, who refuted the *Canon Episcopi* during the thirteenth century. Aquinas strongly disagreed that witchcraft was an illusion, as he was convinced that witches had powers that were given to them by the devil. He believed that not only did witches have the ability to fly through the air, but that they were also capable of shape-shifting, or transforming themselves into animals, birds, insects, or other creatures. Aquinas was also convinced that witches mated with evil spirits, created fierce storms, and used *maleficia*—or evil acts of magic—to cause harm or death to humans, animals, and crops.

Many religious leaders and government officials shared Aquinas's views about witchcraft. In the year 1233 the Christian Church established a formal law-enforcement entity known as

the Inquisition, which empowered designated "inquisitors" with trying, convicting, and executing heretics. At first, people could not be arrested solely on suspicion of witchcraft, but rather, only if they had also committed heresy. But the lines between the two crimes were blurry, and it was not uncommon for suspected witches to be tried and convicted, allegedly for heresy. As the editors of Time-Life Books explain in *Witches and Witchcraft*, "The parallels were only too apparent. It took no great leap of imagination to spot the connection between a devil-worshiping, child-murdering heretic and a night-flying, Satan-loving, sex-crazed sorcerer with a taste for human flesh."[10]

From 1476 to 1834, the Spanish Inquisition tried thousands of accused heretics against the Catholic Church, including witches. This engraving shows victims being burned at the stake.

By the early fourteenth century, the church had expanded the Inquisition's power and had authorized the formal investigation of witchcraft as a crime. With broadened power and authority, the Inquisition began pursuing suspected witches and sorcerers with a vengeance. And while the only characteristic that they all shared in common was being accused of witchcraft, certain factors increased the odds of someone being a suspect. Historian Jenny Gibbons writes, "Most witches were women. Many were poor or elderly; many seem to be unmarried. Most were alienated from their neighbors, or seen as 'different' and disliked."[11] An important factor in the rapid spread of what some historians call *witchcraft madness* was the devastation caused by the bubonic plague, also known as the Black Death. The plague ravaged Europe in the mid-1300s, and by the time the devastating epidemic was over, it had claimed millions of lives—25 to 50 percent of Europe's population died from the disease. Panic was widespread, and it was common for people to assume that witches were responsible for the deaths. Witches were blamed for many other problems as well, such as natural disasters, the failure of crops, lack of rainfall leading to droughts, and every other possible kind of tragedy. Amy Cowles of Johns Hopkins University writes, "Witches were widely believed to be the cause of all the bad things that happened to good people. Faced each day with a hard life in which tragedy was the norm, people needed to blame someone other than God. Accused witches became popular culprits."[12]

"A Thousand Fires"

The Inquisition's pursuit of witches continued to gain strength in the 1400s, and it was given even greater support by the church

in 1484. Two German inquisitors, Heinrich Kramer and Jacob Sprenger, approached Pope Innocent VIII and complained that local religious authorities were interfering with their efforts to prosecute witches. They asked him for help, and he responded by issuing a papal bull called *Summis desiderantes affectibus (Desiring with Supreme Ardor).* The document, as Guiley writes, "granted them full authority to carry out their inquisitions and demanded that they receive whatever support was necessary from local officials."[13] The bull, which promoted the tracking down, torturing, and executing of witches and sorcerers, was

The pursuit of witches across Europe continued to gain strength in the 1400s. For the next 200 years, thousands of accused witches were executed.

Witches and Familiars

Stories about witches often include references to cats because the creatures have been associated with the supernatural since ancient times. Known as *familiars,* witches' cats were said to be possessed by demons, which allowed them to assist with acts of evil magic. Witnesses who testified against convicted English witch Elizabeth Francis claimed that she rewarded her cat, Sathan, with a drop of her blood whenever it performed a task for her. Cats belonging to convicted witches were almost always burned alive so they could do no further harm.

Yet cats were not the only creatures suspected of being familiars. Rabbits, owls, blackbirds, toads, crows, and mice were also believed to assist with witchcraft. Insects that appeared near accused witches were also cause for suspicion, as author Rosemary Ellen Guiley explains: "If a witch was arrested, she was often tied

up and left in a cell, while inquisitors watched secretly to see if her familiars came to her aid. Even an ant or cockroach crawling toward her was called a familiar." Guiley also says that suspicion abounded during witch trials when, "if so much as a fly buzzed in the window while a witch was being questioned or tried, it was said to be her familiar."

Rosemary Ellen Guiley, *The Encyclopedia of Witches and Witchcraft*. New York: Facts On File, 1999.

considered to be one of the most important documents in the history of the church's fight against witchcraft.

The pope furthered the cause by appointing Kramer and Sprenger as his official enforcers. In 1486 the two men published a book called *Malleus Maleficarum*, which translates to *Hammer of the Witches.* One of the passages in the book makes their intention clear: "It has indeed lately come to Our ears . . . [that] many persons of both sexes, unmindful of their own salvation and straying from the Catholic Faith, have abandoned themselves to devils."[14] The book was more than 1,000 pages long, was divided into three separate sections, and included every possible detail that inquisitors would need to know when they investigated witchcraft. In the book's preface, Kramer and Sprenger establish their credibility and reaffirm the authority that had been vested in them by reproducing the entire papal bull written by Pope Innocent. They also include passages from the Bible that support their war on witchcraft.

The focus of part 1 of *Malleus Maleficarum* is on proving that witchcraft and sorcery exist, and it discusses the devil's role in these evil deeds. The book also explains that women, because they are the weaker sex and have an intelligence inferior to men, are naturally more influenced by Satan than are men. Kramer and Sprenger also set out to prove that women are much more wicked than men, and they include biblical quotes to reinforce that opinion. In part 2, the authors describe every possible type of witchcraft, including how witches enter pacts with the devil and the various forms taken by witches, and they also include details about how witches cast malicious spells on people. Part 3 covers detailed instructions for finding witches as well as ways to make them confess their guilt, including various methods of torture. Guiley writes, "Torture is dealt with matter-of-factly; if the accused does not voluntarily confess, even after a year or so in prison, then torture was to be applied as an incentive. Judges are permitted to lie to the accused, promising them mercy if they confess—it is all done in the best interests of society and the state."[15] Part 3 also includes instructions for trying, sentencing, and destroying witches, because the assumed goal is to rid the world of as many of these evil creatures as possible.

Malleus Maleficarum became known as the bible of the witch-hunters. It was reprinted numerous times over the years and was translated from the original Latin into German, French, Italian, and English. The book played a major role in fueling Europe's war on witchcraft, and it played a role in the most massive witch hunt in history. Ruickbie explains, "Kramer and Sprenger had written the textbook for the witch-hunts, and the sparks from their 'Hammer' started a thousand fires across the length and breadth of Europe for the next 200 years."[16]

Chapter 2

Doomed to Die

Although witch hunts were conducted during the latter Middle Ages, the greatest number of executions took place from 1550 to 1650. This was a time of widespread fear and anger as well as a frenzied attempt to stamp out witchcraft at any cost. Not all of Europe was affected by witch-hunting panic; actually, three-fourths of the continent had no witch trials at all. But in areas where witch hunts were common, suspected witches were often arrested and executed based on little or no evidence. Rosemary Ellen Guiley writes, "'Witch' was a devastating accusation. If arrested and taken before a court or inquisitor, one often was assumed to be guilty."[17] This period of hysteria is often called the Burning Times, although convicted witches were often hanged or executed in other ways rather than being burned.

Not all witches were burned at the stake. Other forms of execution were also used, including hanging.

"Torture Is Not to Be Neglected"

In countries such as Germany and France, where the most witch hunts took place, torture methods used against the accused were unbelievably cruel. A strong motivator for inquisitors to use these brutal practices was Kramer and Sprenger's book, *Malleus Maleficarum,* which made it clear that torture was an essential part of the interrogation process. The authors also cautioned that witches who refused to talk after torture were receiving help from the devil, and that he had the power to make a witch "so insensitive to the pains of torture that she will sooner be torn limb from limb [than] confess any of the truth. But torture is not to be neglected for this reason, for they are not all equally endowed with this power."[18]

After witches were captured, arrested, and taken to a prison cell, they were stripped naked and their entire bodies were shaved. Examiners would then check them over carefully in an effort to find the "witch's mark." This could be anything from a small blemish or birthmark to a tiny mole, and it was believed to be the mark of the devil. If such a mark was found, and one usually was, the examiner began sticking pins and needles into it. The common belief was that, through the witch's mark, the devil had given witches an insensitivity to pain. If there was no visible mark, examiners often poked an accused witch's entire body with needles or other sharp objects to see if there was an invisible spot that was not sensitive to pain—again, a sure sign of the devil's work.

Before an accused witch was tortured, he or she was often told what was about to happen and was given the chance to avoid inevitable pain and suffering by confessing. Some feared the torture enough to avoid it by confessing, but most refused because they were not willing to confess to crimes they had not committed. Once torture began, it could take a number of different forms. Victims were whipped with leather straps until they were covered with bleeding welts, or they were brushed with feathers that had been dipped in acid that was strong enough to burn off their flesh. Their skin was burned with red-hot iron rods straight out of a fire, or they were plunged into baths of scalding water. Sometimes people were tortured by having their hands soaked in pots of boiling oil.

There were also numerous instruments that were made for the purpose of torturing the accused. One was known as the thumb-

Before an accused witch was tortured, he or she was often told what was about to happen and was given the chance to avoid inevitable pain and suffering by confessing. This engraving shows the mother of the famous German astronomer, Johannes Kepler, being interrogated for witchcraft in 1615.

screw, which used the great pressure of an iron vise to crush fingers or thumbs. The leg screw worked in a similar way, slowly crushing a person's legs. The *turcas* was used for tearing out fingernails, while the rack stretched victims until their leg and arm joints were pulled apart. Another torture device was the strappado, which was fitted with ropes and a pulley. Victims' hands were tied behind their backs and attached to the pulley, and then they were drawn up toward the ceiling and dropped with such abrupt force that their arms were jerked out of their sockets. To increase the likelihood of pain and physical injury, heavy weights were sometimes put on the victims' feet before they were drawn up in the pulley and dropped.

One of the cruelest methods of punishing accused witches did

Did You Know?

The strappado was a torture device used on witches. Their hands were tied behind their backs and attached to a pulley. Then they were drawn up toward the ceiling and dropped with such abrupt force that their arms were ripped out of their sockets.

not involve torturing them; rather, it forced them to helplessly watch while their loved ones were tortured. In 1594 an accused witch from Scotland named Alison Balfour refused to confess after she had been tortured, so she was forced to watch as torture was used on her husband, son, and seven-year-old daughter. Her grief at watching her family suffer was so great that she quickly confessed, even though she had committed no crime, and she was strangled and then burned at the stake. Such forced confessions often happened when accused witches could no longer endure the suffering. But even if they confessed, they were not necessarily spared further suffering, as Guiley explains: "Victims were usually condemned to death. . . . En route to the gallows or stakes, the condemned were flogged, burned, branded, squeezed with red-hot tongs and subjected to the hacking off of fingers and hands and the cutting out of tongues. The severed body parts were nailed to gallows, a grisly chore that netted the executioner an extra fee."[19]

"He Deserves to Be Burned Alive"

One of the countries where brutal torture methods and witch executions were widespread was France, and there was no shortage of people who were eager to stamp out witchcraft. One of the most zealous of the witch haters was Jean Bodin, a French philosopher who was particularly outspoken about the evils of witches. Bodin was a demonologist, which was the name given to lawyers, judges, and theologians who specialized in exposing witches and their malicious deeds. He was convinced that the authorities were far too soft on the accused, and he often stated that because witches were so evil, they had no legal rights. He also believed that authorities should use whatever methods necessary in order to bring witches to justice. In the mid-1500s Bodin wrote that "not one witch in a million would be accused or punished if the procedure were governed by ordinary rules."[20]

In Bodin's opinion, mere suspicion was more than enough to torment an accused witch because the rumors were generally based in truth. He strongly supported convicting accused witches based on lies by informers, confessions that were made as victims were being tortured, and accusations received by secretive sources. In fact, he encouraged secret accusations by recommending that local authorities place special boxes in their churches where anonymous letters could be deposited—letters that named names and provided the leads he sought. He was outspoken in his belief that witches deserved to be tortured and severely punished for their evil deeds, and he made it clear that no one should be spared from torture, including children, the elderly, or the disabled.

Another French demonologist whose beliefs closely mirrored those of Bodin was Nicholas Remy, a lawyer who also became known for his fight against witchcraft. As a young boy, Remy had been intrigued by the witch trials and executions that took place in villages near his home. When he became an adult, his zealousness toward stamping out witchcraft began after the death of his eldest son. Remy had refused to give money to a beggar woman, and when his son died unexpectedly several days later, he was convinced that the woman was a witch who was responsible for killing his son. Because he was a lawyer, he prosecuted her and had her executed. After that, he committed his time and energy to demonology, believing, like Bodin, that witches were so wicked and evil that they deserved to suffer torture and die painful deaths. Remy often boasted that in the 10-year period between

Jean Bodin was a French philosopher who was particularly outspoken about the evils of witches. Bodin was a demonologist, which was the name given to scholars who specialized in exposing witches.

Did You Know?

In Germany, more accused witches were captured, tortured, and killed than anywhere else in the world.

1581 and 1591, he was personally responsible for 900 accused witches being convicted and burned at the stake. He included that claim in a book that he wrote and published in 1595, which was called *Demonolatry*. It became yet another instructional handbook for people who wanted to bring witches to justice, and it was so popular that it was reprinted eight times.

Tragedy in Bamberg

During the time of Remy and Bodin, witch-hunting in France had reached the point of mass hysteria. The only country in which it was worse was Germany. In fact, there were more accused witches who were captured, tortured, and killed in Germany than anywhere else in the world. Graham Wyley writes that in some German towns, so many people were burned in one day "that the dense, pungent smoke would leave buildings covered in human fat."[21]

One city where violence was rampant was Bamberg, a town located in the German state of Bavaria. Between 1609 and 1623, at least 400 people were executed for witchcraft in Bamberg—and when an official named Gottfried Johann von Dornheim took control, the violence escalated and the executions mounted. Von Dornheim was called Hexenbischof, meaning "witch bishop," and he was known as a fearsome, sadistic ruler who spared the lives of no one accused of being a witch.

Immediately after coming into power, von Dornheim authorized the construction of a witch prison that came to be known as the Witch-House of Bamberg, which, according to Leo Ruickbie, was "furnished with the most extreme instruments of torture imaginable."[22] To help him in his quest to rid the city of witches, von Dornheim created a network of informers and a group of lawyers, torturers, and executioners who would all work together to stamp out Bamberg's witchcraft problem. The operation was a secretive one, whereby the names of the accused were not made public, and they were not allowed to have the assistance of legal counsel in pleading their cases. Under von Dornheim's rule, brutal torture was commonplace, and the accused were regularly burned alive for their alleged crimes. Even people who merely sympathized with the victims were accused of witchcraft and were punished with torture and death.

One of the victims of the Bamberg witch hunt was Johannes Junius, a man who served as an official known as a burgomaster. On June 28, 1628, Junius was arrested on suspicion of being a witch. Although he denied any association with witchcraft, his captors insisted he was lying. They gave him several chances to confess, and when he would not, the torture began. His fingers were crushed in thumbscrews, his legs were crushed in leg screws, and his body was wracked with pain as he was dropped eight times in the strappado. Still, Junius refused to tell his torturers what they wanted to hear, which they took as a sign that he was being aided by the devil. Finally, after a week of unbearable pain and suffering, Junius could take no more—he broke down and made up an elaborate story about his association with the devil. When he had finished talking, his captors were still not satisfied. They took Junius through the streets of Bamberg and ordered him to name others who were also witches. In fear for his life, he gave them names, but when they did not think he had named enough people, they tortured him again.

Junius was sentenced to die and was sent back to his cell. Even though his hands had been crushed, he found the ability to write a letter to his daughter before he was executed. He explained that

Did You Know?

In Bamberg, a town in the German state of Bavaria, a witch prison was built in the early 1600s that came to be known as the Witch-House of Bamberg. It was furnished with the most extreme instruments of torture imaginable.

"QUOTE"

"Innocent have I come into prison, innocent have I been tortured, innocent I must die."

—In 1628, a man accused of witchcraft writing a letter to his daughter about his experience and fate in the witch-house prison.

he had been forced under extreme torture to confess to crimes he had never committed, and he described the methods of torture in detail. He wanted his daughter to understand what had been done to him, and especially to know the truth. He wrote:

> Many hundred thousand good-nights, dearly beloved daughter Veronica. Innocent have I come into prison, innocent have I been tortured, innocent I must die. For whomever comes into the witch prison must become a witch or be tortured until he invents something out of his head. . . . I have taken several days to write this: my hands are both lame. I am in a sad plight. . . . Good night, for your father Johannes Junius will never see you more.[23]

On August 6, 1628, as Junius sat tied to a chair, he was beheaded with a sword, and then his body was burned.

The North Berwick Witches

Witch executions like those in Germany and France were not so common in Scotland. But during the autumn of 1590, a witch hunt began at the command of the Scottish king, James VI. The previous spring the king had wed a young Danish princess named Anne in Norway. On the voyage back to Scotland, the ship had been caught in a terrible storm at sea. To the king's relief, he and his bride made it back to Scotland safely. Yet when he heard that witches were responsible for creating the storm, he vowed to investigate the matter and make those who were guilty pay for what they had done.

James ordered that anyone suspected of being a witch be

brought in for questioning. One of the accused was Agnis Sampson, an old woman who was known for her wisdom as well as for her ability to heal people who were sick. Sampson denied having any involvement with witchcraft, so she was taken away and tortured for refusing to confess. Her captors pinned her to the wall of her cell with an iron contraption known as a witch's bridle, which forced hard, sharp prongs into her tongue and cheeks. They also tortured her by using a method called thrawing, which involved tying ropes around her head and neck and then jerking and twisting them until her skin was raw and bleeding. After days of this brutal treatment and no sleep, Sampson could not take anymore—she broke down and confessed that she was a witch. She began to divulge intricate details to the king about the evil practices she and other witches had participated in. She told of a ritual that they had held in a church in North Berwick, Scotland, where they worshipped the devil and threw a dead cat into the sea. This, according to Sampson, caused the storm that was intended to kill the king and his wife.

In 1590, a witch hunt began at the command of the Scottish king, James VI. Later, he wrote a book called Daemonologie, ***in which he shared his wisdom and knowledge about witchcraft based on his experiences.***

At first, King James was suspicious of the confessions made

by Sampson, referring to her and the other witches as "extreme lyars"[24]—but his views changed when one of the accused allegedly repeated a private conversation he had had with his wife on their wedding night. Sampson was condemned to death; the following January she was strangled, and then her body was thrown into a fire and burned. The other alleged witches were also captured and executed.

In 1597 James wrote a book called *Daemonologie*, in which he shared his wisdom and knowledge about witchcraft based on his experiences. He explained his belief that female witches outnumbered male witches by 20 to 1, but he thought that was because women were frailer and therefore more easily influenced by Satan's power.

A Notorious Witch-Hunter

About 50 years after the king's book was published, it proved to be an inspiration for Matthew Hopkins. Until the mid-1600s Hopkins had never been considered a man of particular importance. Born in Suffolk, England, he had achieved a meager living as a lawyer until the year 1645, when he decided to close his law practice and devote his career to becoming a witch-hunter. He believed this would make him famous as well as allow him to make a better living. He set up headquarters at an inn and advertised that, for a substantial fee, he and his associates would travel to villages, find witches, bring them to trial, and see that they were convicted. To build his importance with the public, Hopkins made false claims about himself, such as saying that he had been appointed to his position by the English Parliament. He also said that he had in his possession a document he called the "Devil's List," which contained the names of all the witches in

England, and he confidently gave himself the title of witch-finder general.

The first victims to fall prey to Hopkins's ruthless witch-hunting spree were elderly women from the towns of Manningtree and Mistley. Hopkins accused them of cursing him with black magic, as Wyley explains: "His allegation was that he had become aware of a coven working in the vicinity who knew of his intentions, so they had sent angry spirits to plague him. One of these spirits was in the form of a giant bear, which was instructed to kill him."[25] The women were subsequently convicted of witchcraft, but they were hanged because witch burning was not considered an accepted method of execution in England.

It was not long before Hopkins was known as a relentless, fearsome, witch-hunter. Along with his associate, John Stearne, as well as several witch-hunting assistants he had hired, Hopkins traveled throughout the English countryside, justifying his outrageous rates by touting his great skills. Wherever he traveled, he succeeded in rounding up dozens of accused witches. As his reputation grew, officials from more towns and villages invited him to visit them, saying that they, too, had witch problems and needed his services. It did not matter to Hopkins that most of the "evidence" he collected was based on gossip, rumors, and false accusations—he believed it was more than enough to accomplish what he had set out to do.

Torture was illegal in England, but that did not stop Hopkins from using his own cruel methods of getting the accused to talk. One of his tactics was to starve his victims, or deprive them of sleep and walk them back and forth in their cells until they were too exhausted to even stand and their feet were swollen and covered with blisters. Often he whipped them in an effort to force

This engraving shows Matthew Hopkins with two women accused of witchcraft. He appointed himself witch-finder general in 1645 and hunted and had executed hundreds of suspected witches in England.

An age which still believed in witch-craft. Two Witches discovered.

a confession, as Wyley writes: "Women were beaten for days on end. Bearing in mind that these were often elderly people, it is not at all surprising that they would confess to anything to put an end to the agony—in fact, death came as a pleasant relief."[26]

If suspected witches still refused to confess, Hopkins used various methods to test their guilt or innocence. One of his favorite tactics was known as witch swimming. Suspects were stripped naked, their hands and feet were tied together, and their bodies were bound with rope so they could not move. Then they were thrown into a river or lake to see whether they would float on the water or sink to the bottom. Wyley explains the reasoning behind this practice: "The idea was that if they sank, they were a good Christian, but if they floated, the water had rejected them and they were identified as a witch. The lame excuse given for this was that the water did not want this impure object floating in it."[27] When accused witches were tested in this way, it was a death sentence for them. They usually drowned, but if they did not, they were executed for having "proven" that they were witches.

Did You Know?

Matthew Hopkins forced children to watch a parent being executed, and because it was believed that witchcraft was hereditary, some of the children were killed too.

Throughout Hopkins's reign as England's most notorious witch-hunter, he reportedly executed more than 230 people whom he had accused of being witches. In one town alone, at least 17 people were hanged in just one day. Children were often forced to watch a parent being executed, and because it was believed that witchcraft was hereditary, some of the children were killed too.

As brutal and cruel as Hopkins's witch-hunting crusade was, it did not last long. Just over a year after he had named himself witch-finder general, his services were no longer in demand and his career came to an abrupt end. Ruickbie explains:

> [Hopkins's] meteoric rise to fame ended in an

The High Cost of Torture

During the height of witch hysteria in Europe, officials in some cities charged fees for the services of the torturers and executioners. Accused witches and their families were expected to pay for the costs involved in brutal torture and death. An itemized chart prepared by an official in Cologne, Germany, is a grim reminder of the barbarous treatment people received when they were accused of being witches and were imprisoned.

> equally rapid, but catastrophic fall from favour. His excessive ambition and enthusiasm in prosecuting witches, although undoubtedly successful, brought criticism of overuse of torture and overcharging of fees. Where before he had been welcomed he found resistance and by 1646 judges and local authorities were beginning to turn against him.[28]

After 1647, the man who was known as the most feared witch-

The items listed include costs for "terrorizing by showing the instruments of torture," "arranging and crushing the thumb," and "beheading and burning, everything included." Others appearing on the list are "for strangling and burning," "burning alive," and "cutting off a hand or several fingers and for beheading all together." Equally as gruesome are categories such as "cutting out the tongue entirely, or part of it, and afterward for burning the mouth with a red-hot iron" and "nailing to the gallows a cut-off tongue or a chopped-off hand."

Editors of Time-Life Books, *Witches and Witchcraft*. Alexandria, VA: Time-Life, 1990.

hunter alive disappeared without a trace. No one knows for sure what happened to him, but there are stories that Hopkins himself was accused of being a witch because of his alleged possession of the Devil's List. He died in 1648, and to this day people can only guess about the cause of his death—but some cannot help wondering if he was tortured and executed like the many victims whose lives he prided himself on ending.

Chapter 3

Witch Hysteria in the New World

During the summer of 1688, something strange and unexplainable occurred in the city of Boston, Massachusetts. Thirteen-year-old Martha Goodwin started having fits of hysteria, screaming words that were gibberish and behaving in bizarre ways that frightened her family. Soon, her brother John, who was 11, began acting in a similar way, as did her younger brother and sister. One minute the children were drenched in sweat and panting as though they were baking inside a hot furnace, and seconds later they were shivering and freezing. They barked like dogs and then purred like cats, and when red streaks mysteriously appeared on their bodies, they said they felt like they were being beaten with invisible sticks. A minister who had observed the children described how terrified and tormented they were, writing that "it would have broke a heart of stone to have seen their agonies."[29] John Goodwin Sr. asked a physician named Thomas Oakes to come to his home and examine his children. When Oakes could find nothing physically wrong with them, he concluded that they were victims of witchcraft.

"A Terror to Evil-Doers"

The Goodwin family immediately suspected their laundress, an Irish slave named Ann Glover, as the person responsible for the bewitchment. Glover was a peculiar-acting older woman who was known for her angry outbursts and strange rantings, and she had been accused in the past of bewitching another woman to death. Martha had recently confronted Glover when she believed the woman had stolen some of the family's linens, and this made Glover furious, causing her to angrily lash out at the girl. Not long after that, Martha and her siblings started having their violent fits, so it was natural that Glover was suspected of bewitching them.

A well-known minister named Cotton Mather heard about the Goodwin children's affliction, and he visited their home to investigate. Like all religious leaders he had known back in England, Mather firmly believed that witches were people who had powers they could only possess if they had made a pact with the devil. He was determined to rid the Goodwin children of the demons that were harming them, and he knew he could only do that if he faced Glover and forced her to confess to her evil acts. As soon as he began questioning her, however, he found that she could only speak Gaelic, the language of her native Ireland. An interpreter was brought in, and after speaking with Glover, he said she had confessed to being a witch.

Glover was arrested and put on trial for the crime of witchcraft, for which she was convicted and condemned to die. On

"QUOTE"

"It would have broke a heart of stone to have seen their agonies"

—In 1688, a minister in Boston who had witnessed what seemed to be two possessed children who were later determined to be victims of witchcraft.

November 16, 1688, she was hanged in the center of town, and her final minutes were described by author James B. Cullen: "She was drawn in a cart, a hated and dreaded figure . . . stared at and mocked at, through the principal streets from her prison to the gallows. . . . The people crowded to see the end, as always; and when it was over they quietly dispersed, leaving the worn-out body hanging as a terror to evil-doers."[30]

"QUOTE"

"When it [the hanging] was over they quietly dispersed, leaving the worn-out body hanging as a terror to evil-doers."

—Author James Cullen describing the hanging of an Irish laundress accused of witchcraft in 1688.

A Frightening Mystery

Just over 3 years later, there was an eerily similar occurrence in a village 17 miles (27km) away from Boston—and it eventually led to the most massive witch hunt in American history. On a cold, dark winter day in January 1692, 2 young girls from the village of Salem were suddenly stricken with a frightening ailment. One of the girls, Elizabeth "Betty" Parris, was the 9-year-old daughter of the Reverend Samuel Parris, and the other was Abigail Williams, Betty's 11-year-old cousin. For no apparent reason, they began having violent fits, uttering weird noises, cursing God, and screaming abusive tirades in a language that no one could understand. They suffered from convulsions and odd skin sensations, and they were found crawling into holes and contorting their bodies in unnatural ways. At times they were completely delirious and hallucinating; at other times, they just stared blankly as though they were in trances. John Hale, a minister who witnessed their behavior, described it by saying it was as if the children were being "pinched and bitten by invisible agents; their arms, necks, and backs turned this way and that, and returned back again. . . . Sometimes they were [mute], their mouths stopped, their throats choked, their limbs wracked and tormented."[31] Before long, other girls and young women in Salem began to exhibit similar behavior, which prompted physician William Griggs to declare that their mysterious afflictions were caused by the evils of witchcraft. Word of the girls' bewitchment spread fast, and the people of Salem began to panic—they desperately wanted the witches found so no one else could be harmed by them. Mary Sibley, the aunt of one of the girls, decided to use magic to find out who the witches were. She believed that a "witch cake" should be baked using rye flour and the girls' urine, which would then be fed to a dog. She believed that if the girls were truly bewitched, the animal would either erupt into fits or it would lead them to the witches who were responsible for the evil acts. Sibley asked a woman named Tituba, a Caribbean slave who was owned by the Parris family, to bake the witch cake for her. But when Reverend Parris heard what Sibley had done, he was outraged, accusing her of tapping into satanic powers in order to fight the devil. He gave Sibley a harsh reprimand for becoming involved in such a sinful activity, and he publicly humiliated her in church. He also issued a warning to the congregation about the dangers that were ahead, shouting from the pulpit that the devil had been raised among them, that his rage was terrible, and that only God knew when and if his evils would be silenced.

As though Parris had touched a match to a field of dry brush, he set off a massive fire of fear and suspicion that spread through the village. Everyone in Salem was caught up in the antiwitchcraft hysteria, as author and historian Marc Aronson explains:

> In the early months of 1692 many in Salem were so on edge that what people saw as accusations of witchcraft, manifestations of witchcraft, and devilish misinformation about witchcraft all blended

Did You Know?

The event in American history that came to be known as the Salem Witch Trials began on a cold, dark winter day in January 1692. Two young girls from the village of Salem, Massachusetts were suddenly stricken with a frightening ailment that led to accusations of witchcraft.

> together and confirmed one another's reality. Everywhere you turned, there was more evidence that the devil was nearby, even in the spread of lies and half-truths. Everything seemed covered in a [cloud] of deceit—the devil's trait—and there was no apparent way out but to find the witches, the devil's agents, execute them, and return the community to safety in the sight of God. . . . The eerie powers of the invisible realm seemed to be manifesting themselves everywhere, too real to ignore.[32]

In February 1692 Betty Parris and Abigail Williams revealed the name of the first witch who they said had cast spells on them: Tituba, the Parris's slave. As the girls sobbed and wailed uncontrollably, they said that she "did pinch, prick, and grievously torment them."[33] But their accusations did not stop with Tituba. They went on to claim that two elderly women named Sarah Good and Sarah Osborne were also witches. Within days of the accusations, the three women were arrested and taken to Salem officials for questioning—and the witchcraft hysteria in Salem began to escalate rapidly.

"Conspiracy of Evil Forces"

Betty and Abigail attended the pretrial questioning session, as did two other girls who claimed they were bewitched, Ann Putnam Jr. and Elizabeth Hubbard. The public was invited to attend the hearing, and villagers flocked to the meetinghouse to watch the proceedings. Because Tituba was a slave from a mysterious, faraway land, people were automatically suspicious of her. Good and

A Caribbean slave named Tituba is pictured here telling tales to children. She was accused of being a witch and casting spells on children.

Osborne were also considered probable witches because they were poor elderly women who did not attend church, and they were not highly regarded by the other villagers.

Good was the first to be questioned by magistrates John Hathorne and Jonathan Corwin, and she promptly denied having any association with witchcraft. Her words of denial immediately caused the four girls to dissolve into a rash of convulsive fits. Upon seeing what appeared to be great agony, Hathorne and Corwin angrily demanded that Good explain why she would cause innocent girls to suffer in that way. She continued to insist that she was free from guilt, but then she turned on Osborne, saying the woman was a witch and was likely responsible for what had happened to the girls. Osborne was questioned next,

What Really Happened?

No one knows for sure why the people of Salem, Massachusetts, were so consumed with witch-hunting hysteria. It all started with the strange afflictions of the girls who were said to be bewitched. Behavioral scientist Linnda Caporeal has a theory about what was wrong with them: poisoning by a fungus called ergot. Caporeal studied witch trial records and the diaries of Salem residents, and she learned that the girls' symptoms included delusions, hallucinations, crawling sensations on the skin, violent muscle spasms, and con-

and she denied what Good had said about her—and once again, the four girls erupted into uncontrollable hysteria, this time wailing that "the woman's specter [ghost] was roaming the room, biting them, pinching them and often appearing as a bird or other animal someplace in the room."[34]

Tituba was the last of the three to be questioned. At first she denied any wrongdoing, saying she had never harmed the girls in any way and had much affection for them. Then, to the shock vulsions—all of which are symptoms of ergot poisoning. The fungus can infect cereal grasses such as rye, and it thrives in areas that have warm, rainy springs and summers. Those conditions were present in Salem during the growing season of 1691, so the village was an ideal breeding ground for the fungus. Rye was the people's staple grain, and if the rye consumed during the early months of 1692 was contaminated by the fungus, ergot poisoning could have caused the girls' ailments. That alone cannot explain the hysteria because, after the first reports of "bewitchment," the situation spun out of control. Still, Caporeal believes the possible connection between the ergot fungus and the Salem witch persecutions is too fascinating a theory to ignore.

of everyone in attendance, Tituba's testimony abruptly changed. Perhaps because she knew the court would be more lenient toward someone who confessed to being a witch, she said that the devil had asked her to serve him, and that he was to blame for causing her to hurt the girls. She went on to tell an elaborate tale of her involvement in witchcraft, including her assertion that Good and Osborne were witches who had forced her to attack Ann Putnam Jr. with a knife. She said she was sorry for the

Did You Know?

During the Salem Witch Trials, a 12-year-old girl named Ann Putnam Jr., told officials that the ghosts of murdered people appeared to her every night, giving her information about who was responsible for their deaths.

evil acts she had committed, and she would never harm anyone again. Then she went further, surprising her questioners by saying that the witchcraft went far beyond Salem, and that there was an entire coven of witches in Massachusetts.

At the end of the questioning session, the three women were taken to prison to await their formal trial. Because of the detailed story Tituba had told, there was no longer any doubt that Salem was threatened by witchcraft. The villagers were now more certain than ever that evil forces were in their midst, and they wanted them destroyed.

A Growing Witch List

During the following weeks, other girls and young women in Salem began to come forward, claiming that they too were victims of bewitchment. The most highly detailed, dramatic stories were given by 12-year-old Ann Putnam Jr., who told officials that the ghosts of murdered people appeared to her every night, giving her information about who was responsible for their deaths. She also said that spirits of live witches often tormented her, such as when the specter of a villager named Elizabeth Proctor had attacked her, biting and pinching her and trying to get her to sign the devil's book that would make her become a witch too. Putnam also claimed that the spirit of Sarah Good's deceased daughter had attached itself to her throat, nearly choking her, and that she also had tried to force Putnam to sign the book of evil. Because of her elaborate tales of bewitchment, Putnam achieved near-celebrity status. As young as she was, she found herself at the center of Salem's witch-hunting hysteria.

As the town became more and more obsessed with finding witches, Putnam and her mother, Ann Putnam Sr., became Salem's leading witch accusers. The first person they named was Martha Corey, which stunned villagers because she was a respectable church-going woman who was highly regarded by those who knew her. When Corey was first questioned about her involvement with witchcraft, she swore that it was not true. She wanted to talk with young Ann about why she would make such an accusation, so she went to the Putnam home. But her visit was far different from what she had hoped. As soon as the girl saw her, she began behaving wildly, acting as though she were suffocating and choking, twisting her hands and feet in unnatural ways, and claiming that she had a vision of Corey's specter roasting a man over a fire. Soon afterward, Corey was arrested and taken to the magistrates for questioning.

Giles Corey (holding hat) was one of several men in Salem accused of witchcraft and was executed by being crushed by boulders.

Corey's pretrial was held on March 21, 1692. As with the hearings of Tituba, Good, and Osborne, curious people filled the meetinghouse so they could watch the proceedings. Ann Putnam Jr. was among the attendees, as were 9 others who were allegedly bewitched by Corey, including 4 adult women and 3 female servants. Because of Corey's high standing in the community, fellow church members and village officials did not want the accusations against her to be true. She stood before the magistrates and denied the charges, pleading with them to believe her. "I am an innocent person," she cried. "I never had to do with witchcraft since I was born. I am a Gospel Woman."[35] But as soon as she denied her guilt, the girls and young women who had accused her began to lash out, howling as though in pain and screaming accusations at her. No matter how respectable Corey was in the village, everyone who witnessed the girls' bizarre behavior believed that she had harmed them, including Corey's 80-year-old husband, Giles Corey, who asked that she confess to being a witch. Corey found that she was up against a force that was far greater than her own power, and after the session was over, she was taken to prison to await her trial.

Over the following weeks, more accused witches were arrested and taken to the magistrates for questioning. They came from all walks of life and ranged in age from young to old. And while most of the accused were women, there were also several men who were charged, including Giles Corey and John Proctor, whose wife, Elizabeth, was also one of the accused. Suddenly it was obvious that no one in Salem was safe from being branded a witch, as Aronson explains: "The game was now completely out of control. The accusers either were carrying out a malicious plot that drew in more and more conspirators or were in a highly charged state of mind in which each backed up and further excited the others. There was no truth except their passion to be heard and their drive to expand their range of destruction."[36] By mid-May nearly 30 people were in Boston jails for committing crimes of witchcraft, and it appeared that the madness was never going to end.

This wood carving, "Accusation of the Witch," hangs in the Essex Institute in Salem, Massachusetts, symbolizing the horror that swept through the town in 1692.

"I Am No Witch"

As the number of accused witches continued to grow, a formal ruling body was needed to preside over their impending trials. William Phips, the governor of Massachusetts, publicly stated that the colony was "miserably harassed with a most horrible witchcraft,"[37] and he vowed that the evildoers would be brought to justice. He appointed nine men to serve as judges on the court of Oyer and Terminer ("to hear and determine"), and Hathorne and Corwin were among them. The first trial of the new court was held on June 2, 1692. The accused witch, a woman named Bridget Bishop, was found guilty and was condemned to die, even though she pleaded with the judges and insisted she was wrongly accused. "I am no witch," she cried. "I am innocent. I know nothing of it."[38] Bishop's pleas were ignored, however, and eight days later she was hanged from trees on Salem's Gallow's Hill. On that day, she became the village's first person to be executed for the crime of witchcraft.

Following Bishop's death, several people spoke out in protest, expressing their belief that the witch trials were unjust and innocent people were being killed. Some of them signed petitions on behalf of accused villagers they believed were being wrongly accused. One of the court's judges, Nathaniel Saltonstall, agreed that Bishop had been executed based on little or no evidence, and he showed his disgust by resigning from the court. Their protests were ignored, however, and the number of accusations and arrests continued to escalate.

In this Salem cemetery, the second oldest in the United States, are the graves of witch trial judges John Hathorne and Jonathan Corwin.

Over the next months there were more trials, more guilty verdicts, and more executions. The number of people who claimed to be victims of bewitchment had swelled, and the evidence against the accused witches was still based solely on the hysterical actions of the young accusers. "By now," writes Rosemary Ellen Guiley, "the girls' power was so great that they were celebrities in the colony and believed invincible. Consequently, citizens of neighboring towns requested that the girls look at their communities with their spectral vision and find the witches responsible for whatever problems existed: illness, poor crops, dead livestock."[39]

One nearby town that asked for help was Andover, which was 11 miles (18km) from Salem. Officials in Andover were concerned that witchcraft might be causing problems in their town as well, and they asked for help in exposing the evil creatures. Abigail Williams, Ann Putnam Jr., Elizabeth Hubbard, and a few other girls stated their belief that Andover was filled with witches, and more than 40 of them were identified. One of the accused was Martha Carrier, a woman from Andover who was tried and condemned in the Salem court for witchcraft in early August. At her trial, Carrier swore that she was innocent, which caused the girls to react as they had so many times before—by screaming and howling as though they were suffering from unbearable pain. Aronson explains, "The judge believes the young women are under demonic attack and uses their agonies to press Martha to confess her own sin. But Martha, stoic, almost disdainful in her calm disgust, sees only lies."[40] Based on the girls' hysterical actions, Carrier was found guilty and was condemned to die. On August 19 she was hanged on Gallow's Hill along with four other convicted witches.

Eventually the witch trials came to be looked upon as a tragic mistake. Pictured is a high priestess at the Witch Trials Memorial who supports the drive pressuring lawmakers to clear the names of those falsely accused and executed for witchcraft in Salem.

By the end of September 1692 the statistics of the Salem witch hunt were staggering: More than 100 people had been imprisoned, and 19 people had been hanged, including 13 women and 6 men. Among the dead was Sarah Osborne, 1 of the first 3 women to be accused of witchcraft, who was in such frail health that she had died in prison within 2 months of being sent there. Giles Corey was among the executed, but he was not hanged like the others. After refusing to participate in a trial, he was taken to a field in Salem, staked to the ground, and covered with large wooden planks. Heavy boulders were then piled on top of the planks, 1 at a time, until Corey was slowly crushed to death.

The Hysteria Comes to an End

As the toll of accused witches who were imprisoned and executed continued to rise, increasing numbers of people feared that the convicted were being charged based on false evidence and that innocent people were dying. Even those who had long been dedicated to witch-hunting were questioning how there could be such large numbers of witches in such a small colony as Massachusetts. Then, on October 3, 1692, one of the colony's most prominent religious leaders, Increase Mather, the father of Cotton Mather, published a written statement that spoke out against the Salem witch trials. He wrote that in spite of the hysterical fits, in spite of the spectral appearances that the girls had claimed to see, it was all the devil's work and therefore was not to be trusted. "To take away the life of anyone," he wrote, "merely because a specter or Devil, in a bewitched or possessed person does accuse them, will bring the guilt of innocent blood on the land. . . . It were better that ten suspected witches should escape than that one innocent person should be condemned."[41]

Because of public pressure and growing suspicion that the witch trials had been a tragic mistake, Governor Phips dissolved the court of Oyer and Terminer at the end of October. He then created a new Supreme Court to try the remaining cases of accused people who were still being held in prison. With the new court in place, and new rules that made spectral evidence inadmissible, juries acquitted almost all of the accused. Only three more people were found guilty of witchcraft, and all three were later pardoned.

In 1697 the Reverend John Hale, a former supporter of the witch trials, wrote his regrets about what had happened in Salem. He said that even though he believed the people who were involved in the cases meant well, "such was the darkness of that day, the tortures and lamentations of the afflicted, and the power of former [precedents], that we walked in the clouds and could not see our way."[42]

Did You Know?

In 1697 the Reverend John Hale, a former supporter of the witch trials, wrote his regrets about what had happened in Salem. Even today there is a movement to exonerate those who were tried and executed as witches.

CHAPTER 4

"An' It Harm None"

The religion known as Wicca is not well understood, nor is it easy to define. It is sometimes called the religion of witchcraft because many people of the Wicca faith (known as Wiccans) call themselves witches. Yet there are other Wiccans who do not consider themselves witches and who never practice witchcraft. Even though the words *Wicca* and *witchcraft* are often used interchangeably, they are not the same thing. The biggest difference is that whereas all Wiccans worship one or more deities, witches may or may not be religious. Some are atheists, meaning they do not recognize any deities at all. Others consider themselves agnostics, or people who neither believe nor disbelieve in the existence of gods or goddesses.

Gwinevere Rain, a Wiccan who wrote the book *Confessions of a Teenage Witch*, shares her perspective about the religion she has chosen to embrace:

Here a witch flying on her broomstick carries a child intended as a sacrifice. Wiccans complain they are often associated with such images and horrific practices; however, they stress that the Wiccan religion simply strives for self-growth through meditation and positive spells.

There are several main stereotypes associated with Wicca: that we perform blood sacrifices, fly on broomsticks, or want to curse everyone. Wiccans don't participate in any of those events. Instead, we seek to grow as individuals, using prayer, meditation, creative visualization, and positive spells to improve our lives. Each day Wiccans continually try to combat negative projection and seek to show the path in its true light.[43]

A "Long, Tangled History"

Wicca is a neopagan religion—which means it is based on modern pagan (earth-centered) beliefs—and of all the religions that exist today, there is none with a history more hotly debated among its followers. Some Wiccans refer to their faith as the Old Religion because they are convinced that it is a direct descendant of an ancient religion that has existed for thousands of years. That has largely been disproved over time, however. Even though many Wiccan beliefs are modeled after pagan religions of ancient Europe, there is no historical evidence to support that Wicca itself is a remnant of ancient times. In fact, historians say there was no organized religion in Europe at all before Christianity. According to Kaatryn MacMorgan, who is a member of the Church of Universal Eclectic Wicca, the religion has a "long, tangled history. . . . Wicca is not the modern practice of the ancient religion of one group of people, instead, it combines portions of many different religious beliefs from many different European tribes with many of the rational ideas that have evolved in the past two hundred years."[44]

The late Gerald Gardner, who is said to be the founder of the modern Wiccan religion, did not agree with that viewpoint. He was convinced that Wicca was a direct descendant of the Old Religion. Gardner was a civil servant from Great Britain and an avid follower of Margaret Murray, who was a noted anthropologist and author. Murray believed that there was a direct line from a pagan religion of 25,000 years ago to the witchcraft of her time. In Gardner's book *Witchcraft Today,* which was published in 1954, he expresses support for Murray's philosophies, writing that not only was witchcraft a religion, but it was also an ancient pagan religion that had existed since long before Christianity. "What Margaret Murray has theorized is quite true," he writes. "Witchcraft *was* a religion and, in fact, it still is. I know, because I am a Witch myself."[45] Gardner claimed that the reason witchcraft had managed to survive in spite of the witch persecutions in Europe was because its practitioners were highly secretive about their covens as well as about their beliefs and rituals. He was convinced that witchcraft was very much alive; it was just being hidden from public view.

Gardner had originally developed an interest in witchcraft a number of years before he wrote and published *Witchcraft Today.* According to Gardner, he was initiated into the Old Religion in 1939 by a witch named Dorothy Clutterbuck, who was the high priestess of a coven known as New Forest. Over the following years, Gardner collected a vast amount of knowledge about ancient folklore, magic, and witchcraft. He wanted to write about what he had learned so he could share his knowledge with others who were also fascinated by witchcraft. At that time, however, there were strict antiwitchcraft laws in Great Britain, which forced him to remain secretive about his beliefs. In 1949 he wrote about them in a novel called *High Magic's Aide,* but he kept his identity hidden by publishing the book under the penname of "Scire."

In 1951 the last of Great Britain's witchcraft laws were finally repealed, and Gardner no longer had to hide his involvement with the craft. He remained with the New Forest coven until 1951, then broke away from the group, formed his own coven, and wrote *Witchcraft Today.* The book was immensely successful and influential among witchcraft practitioners, and it led to the formation of numerous covens throughout England. It also turned Gardner into a celebrity who was often called "Britain's Chief Witch" by

Did You Know?

Wicca is a neopagan religion—which means it is based on modern pagan (earth-centered) beliefs—and of all the religions that exist today, there is none with a history more hotly debated among its followers.

the media. The religion that he had founded came to be known as Wicca, and the branch that remained loyal to Gardner's core beliefs was called Gardnerian Wicca.

In the early 1960s Gardner met Raymond Buckland, who had moved to the United States from his native England. The two began corresponding, and Buckland was eventually initiated into Gardner's coven by a high priestess known as Lady Olwen. It was Buckland who introduced Wicca to America, and because of his efforts, the popularity of the religion grew quickly. He explains, "At that time there were no covens visible in this country. Initiated in Scotland . . . I set out to emulate Gardner insofar as to try to straighten out long-held misconceptions and to show the Craft for what it truly is. . . . It was an exciting time as more and more covens, and many different traditions, came into the open or at least made themselves known."[46] In 1973 Buckland perceived what he saw as power struggles and corruption, as well as favoritism of male deities over female ones, within the Gardnerian group. As a result, he split to form his own branch of Wicca.

The Wiccan Rede

In the years since the Wiccan religion first started to become popular, it has evolved and changed a great deal—so much so that there are vast differences in beliefs among Wiccans. Unlike Christianity or other organized religions whose followers rely on holy books for guidance, there is no such universal guide for Wiccans; neither are there any well-defined guidelines about practicing the religion. A Wiccan author who goes by the name of Starhawk appreciates that characteristic about Wicca, explaining that it "is not based on dogma or a set of beliefs, nor on scriptures, or a sacred book revealed by a great man. Witchcraft

Pictured is a Wiccan high priestess standing at an altar displaying the tools of witchcraft magic and power. The biggest difference between Wiccans and witches is all Wiccans worship one or more deities while witches may or may not be religious.

takes it teachings from nature and reads inspiration in the movements of the sun, moon and stars, in the flight of birds, in the slow growth of trees and in the cycles of the seasons."[47]

Many Wiccans share Starhawk's viewpoint, enjoying the loosely knit principles of their religion and viewing the differences as part of its appeal. Just as people of different Christian denominations hold differing viewpoints, these Wiccans see no reason why people of their faith should all be exactly the same. But for some followers of Wicca, the religion's lack of clear definition and direction is far from positive, and they are troubled by it. Catherine Noble Beyer writes, "There is no solid definition of Wicca. Many Wiccans consider that a bonus, and they shouldn't. It's a serious, serious problem. A religion is a set of common beliefs. Without definition, the term 'Wicca' becomes meaningless. . . . Words without definition become nonsense."[48]

Even in the absence of an official creed or well-defined set of guidelines, one thing that draws Wiccans together is a basic principle or law known as the Wiccan Rede. No one knows exactly where the principle came from or how old it is, but it has been around at least since Gardner popularized the Wiccan religion and possibly before that. Over the years the Wiccan Rede has become an important moral focus for people of the Wiccan community, as Rain explains: "Our Rede. . . is the foundation of Wicca. It is one small phrase with powerful and breathtaking meaning. Despite all the different traditions and eclectic ways, it is this rule that unites us."[49] The heart of the Wiccan Rede is an eight-word passage that says, "An' it harm none, do what thou wilt" or "do what ye will."

Even though all Wiccans abide by the Wiccan Rede, they often disagree about what it is intended to mean. Whereas some believe it is a directive that they are never allowed to cause harm to anyone or anything, others say it does not mean that at all. MacMorgan explains:

> The Wiccan Rede DOES NOT mean that one must tiptoe through life afraid to accidentally cause harm. The use of "an'" is very deliberate, and in Modern English is closer to "as long as." . . . Put in modern words and form, the Rede says "If an action will cause no harm do it freely, but if it has the capacity to harm, use your religious and other experiences to decide the best course of action that causes the least amount of harm to yourself and others.[50]

In spite of the fact that Wiccans have different interpretations of the Rede, they still consider it basic moral guidance for their lives.

Core Beliefs

In addition to following the Wiccan Rede, there are core beliefs that most Wiccans share, which bind them together as a diverse, but still united, religious group. One of the most fundamental beliefs is their worship of deities. For most Wiccans this includes both a god and a goddess, which Rain describes as "dual, two halves of a whole and work as complementary equals. . . . We can find them not in a distant unreachable heaven, but in nature and deep within ourselves."[51] Most Wiccans worship their gods and goddesses with equal reverence, although some place greater importance on one than the other.

There is a very close connection between the deities who are worshipped and Wiccans' deep respect for nature and all living things. Beyer explains, "As embodiments of the universe, the God and Goddess dwell everywhere and are within everything. This means that while they are many beautiful and bountiful things, they are also the raging storm, the thundering earth, and the sweeping fire. They are joyous birth and wasting disease, because all are part of the natural cycle of life."[52]

Wiccans also abide by another core belief known as the Law of Return, which is sometimes called the Rule of Three or the Threefold Law. It is an extension of the Wiccan Rede and serves as a reminder that whatever energy people send out or whatever actions they take (whether positive or negative), will eventually return to them three times over. The belief is sometimes referred to as the Wiccan version of the Christian golden rule, "Do unto others as you would have them do unto you." Loosely translated, the Law of Return means that if Wiccans do good things in their lives, they will be rewarded with good, and if they choose to do evil, then they can expect to receive evil as their reward.

Did You Know?

The Law of Return, which is a part of the Wiccan Rede, states that whatever energy people send out or whatever actions they take (whether positive or negative), will eventually return to them three times over.

Wiccan Traditions

The Wiccan Rede and core beliefs provide general guidance for people who practice the Wiccan religion, but the various denominations and branches, known as traditions, all have their own sets of beliefs and practices. Even Wiccans within a particular tradition may have vastly different beliefs from others who are part of the same tradition. This dissimilarity has become even more obvious as new traditions have continued to form and as Wicca has grown more popular. Some well-known traditions include Alexandrian Wicca, Celtic Wicca, Blue Star Wicca, Faery Wicca, and Traditional Wicca.

Gardnerian Wicca is the dominant tradition worldwide. It is centered on a worship of the goddess and the horned god, deities who are represented by a high priestess and high priest. "Nature is honored," writes Rosemary Ellen Guiley, "and one accepts oneself and all other living things as part of her. . . . Formal initiation into a coven by a high priest or high priestess is stressed. . . . One enters the coven in 'perfect love and perfect trust,' which means complete trust of fellow coveners. A woman must be initiated into a coven by a man, and vice versa."[53] Raymond Buckland brought Gardnerian Wicca to America and was a member of it until he founded his own Seax Wicca tradition.

Like other Wicca traditions, the Church of Universal Eclectic Wicca (CUEW) follows the Wiccan Rede adhering to the Law of Return, as well as the Ethic of Self-Responsibility, which is a belief that if things go wrong, the Wiccan assumes responsibility rather than placing blame elsewhere. Members worship deities that are genderless as well as male and female deities whom they refer to as the Lord and Lady. Leaders of the CUEW tradition believe in searching for the truth in many different places, and they encourage members to experiment and explore their religious faith, holding on to things that work for them and letting go of things that do not. These Wiccans often use the phrase "Whatever works!" to describe their religious journeys, but they are careful to define what they mean by that: "When we say 'Whatever Works' it does not mean just grab any old thing and the kitchen sink, put it together and call it Wicca if it feels good to you. We mean what works for you after careful evaluation, study and experimentation within the context of Wicca."[54]

Some Wiccans belong to no tradition or group of any kind. Instead, they practice their religion individually, which is what

Rain chooses to do. Because she also uses witchcraft, she refers to herself as a solitary Wiccan witch, as she describes how this differs from Wiccans who belong to organized groups:

> Years ago it was believed that the only way to join Wicca was to be initiated by another practitioner. Within the past two decades this thought pattern has changed dramatically. Some solitary practitioners use self-initiation rituals and others like myself see no need to have any sort of initiation. You are a Wiccan through practice, honoring the Wiccan Rede and having true knowledge of the Craft.[55]

"QUOTE"

"You are a Wiccan through practice, honoring the Wiccan Rede and having true knowledge of the Craft."

— Gwinevere Rain, author of *Confessions of a Teenage Witch,* describing how today anyone can be a Wiccan without the traditional initiation process.

A Time to Celebrate

Whether Wiccans practice on a solitary basis or as part of a tradition, they use a calendar that is known as the Wheel of the Year. This colorful wheel represents the eternal cycle of life and signifies that the cycle of seasons is endlessly turning. Spaced around the Wiccan wheel are eight special holidays known as sabbats, which mark important seasonal transitions for Wiccans. It is when they pay tribute to higher powers by giving thanks for the many bounties of the earth and nature. And while Wiccans may celebrate the sabbats in their own special ways, using different kinds of rituals, the holidays are joyous times that often involve festivals with feasting, music, dancing, and laughter.

The first day of the Wiccan year is the sabbat of Yule. It falls on the longest night of the year, known as the winter solstice, and occurs anytime between December 20 and 23. Wiccans observe Yule as the day that the goddess gives birth to the sun god, and it is when they celebrate the start of the Sun's return. To welcome the Sun, they light fires or candles, and they decorate with holly and mistletoe.

The next sabbat is Imbolc, or the Feast of Lights. It is celebrated on February 2 and is considered to be a time when the goddess has recovered from childbirth and the earth is renewing itself. For Wiccans, Imbolc is a time to celebrate the first signs that spring will once again return. The next month they celebrate Ostara, which is the time of the spring equinox, or the official start of spring. Ostara occurs on March 21, and it represents a new beginning for Wiccans because days start to become longer and nights become shorter. Ostara is thought to be the time when the goddess has awakened and is blessing the earth with fertility, and Wiccans celebrate by coloring eggs and planting seeds in the fertile earth.

The sabbat Beltane occurs on May 1 and is also called May Day. It is when Wiccans celebrate the end of the planting season and the beginning of what is sure to be a plentiful harvest as well as a continuation of the wheel-of-life cycle. There are often glorious flower festivals on Beltane, when Wiccans dance around decorated maypoles to celebrate fertility.

The longest day of the year, June 22, is known as the summer solstice and the time of Litha, one of the most important Wiccan holidays. Extravagant Litha festivals are held in Europe and other parts of the world to honor the deities, and Guiley explains what these celebrations are like: "A bit of madness is in the air. Great bonfires are lit to help the sun change its course in the sky. . . . Burning wheels are rolled downhill, and burning disks are hurled at the sun. . . . Celebrants jump over fires."[56] Many Wiccan weddings are held during Litha, and the newlyweds jump over a

Did You Know?

The longest day of the year, June 22, is known as the summer solstice and the time of Litha, one of the most important Wiccan holidays.

broom to celebrate their new union.

A sabbat on August 1 is known as Lughnasadh (pronounced "loon-sar"), which is named for Lugh, the Irish Celtic solar god. It is a time when Wiccans celebrate the harvesting of fruits and grains and the approach of the fall months. Then, on September 21, autumn arrives with the autumnal equinox, and Wiccans celebrate Mabon. The hours of day and night are equal on this day, so the sabbat represents the balance between light and dark. And when the days begin to get shorter and the nights grow longer, the end of the Wiccan year has arrived, bringing a sabbat known as Samhain (pronounced "soe-en"). It falls on October 31 and is sometimes called All Hallow's Eve or, as it is more commonly known, Halloween.

A Misunderstood Faith

Whenever Wiccans celebrate their sabbats or perform any types of rituals, they often practice their faith in secret. Although archaic witchcraft laws disappeared long ago and Wicca is more accepted today than it has been in the past, there is still a great deal of misinformation about it. People often think of Wicca as an evil religion that is based on devil worship, even though this is not part of Wiccan beliefs or practices. Wiccans do not believe in the existence of an evil deity known as the devil or Satan, and they do not believe there is a place called hell. That is why it is inaccurate for them to be called devil worshippers—it is impossible for them to worship something whose existence they do not recognize. The fear of being associated with satanic beliefs often forces Wiccans to hide their faith, even from their friends and family. If they do decide to reveal themselves, they often refer to it as "coming out of the broom closet."

A Victory for Wiccans

In September 2005 National Guard sergeant Patrick Stewart of Fernley, Nevada, was killed when the helicopter he was flying in was shot down over Afghanistan. Stewart was a Wiccan, and his wife wanted a five-pointed star enclosed in a circle, known as a pentacle, to be inscribed on his marker on the Veteran's Memorial Wall. U.S. Department of Defense officials refused her request because the pentacle was not an approved religious symbol for military markers—even though the government agency had approved the symbols of nearly forty other faiths, including various versions of the Christian cross, the Jewish Star of David, the Muslim crescent, the Buddhist wheel, the Mormon angel, the nine-pointed star of the religion called Baha'i, and even a symbol for atheists. After a battle that lasted more than a year, the government finally granted Roberta Stewart's request. In April 2007 she was given permission for the pentacle to be added to her husband's marker, and it also became an approved religious symbol for other Wiccan soldiers.

Margot Adler is a high priestess with the Gardnerian tradition. Like all Wiccans, Adler encounters prejudice by people who do not understand her religion, and she offers an explanation that she hopes will help them learn to be more tolerant:

> We are not evil. We don't harm or seduce people. We are not dangerous. We are ordinary people like you. We have families, jobs, hopes, and dreams. We are not a cult. This religion is not a joke. We are not what you think we are from looking at T.V. We are real. We laugh, we cry. We are serious. We have a sense of humor. You don't have to be afraid of us. We don't want to convert you. And please don't try to convert us. Just give us the same right we give you—to live in peace. We are much more similar to you than you think.[57]

"QUOTE"

"We are not evil. We don't harm or seduce people. We are not dangerous. We are ordinary people like you."

— A Wiccan high priestess explaining that Wiccans only want to be respected by society and live in peace.

CHAPTER 5

Modern Witchcraft

Witchcraft is very much alive today, and the witches who practice it do not necessarily stand out in a crowd. In fact, most witches look and act just like everyone else, as Raymond Buckland writes: "You do not have to be born on Halloween to be a Witch. You do not have to have a five-pointed star in the lines of your hand to be a Witch. You do not have to be the seventh child of a seventh child to be a Witch. Nor do you have to wear strange robes, or be naked, wear lots and lots of jewelry, or paint your fingernails black to be a Witch. Witches are ordinary people."[58] The men who practice witchcraft are called witches, not warlocks. Actually, the word *warlock* is a derogatory term because it means "oath breaker." It was used during the European witch hunts to refer to people who betrayed other witches, and it still has a negative perception among practicing witches.

Did You Know?

Modern day witches do not necessarily stand out in a crowd. In fact, most witches look and act just like everyone else.

People become witches in a number of different ways. Some are known as hereditary witches, meaning they were born with the powers of witchcraft because their ancestors before them were witches. Other people make a conscious decision to become witches, perhaps because they believe they have psychic abilities or because they are dissatisfied with traditional religion and are seeking new answers for their lives. They may study witchcraft and practice it on their own, or they may approach a coven and ask to be admitted. If the coven agrees, there is usually a waiting period of a year or more before the aspiring witch is allowed to participate in a formal initiation process. Seasoned witches want to be sure that aspiring witches take their commitment to the craft very seriously before they become part of a coven.

From Wiccan Witches to Powwowing

Witchcraft is practiced all over the world in many different forms. Traditional witches are often confused with Wiccans, and although they may practice similar rituals and observe some of the same holidays, their core beliefs are quite different. Traditional witches believe in the existence of deities, but they do not regard gods and goddesses as supreme beings, nor do they worship them. They have reverence for nature and feel a strong spiritual connection to it, and they pay tribute to seasonal changes such as full moons and summer and winter solstices, but it is nature itself that they honor, not the gods and goddesses associated with it. And although most traditional witches follow their own rules about personal responsibility and honor, they do not abide by moral codes such as the Wiccan Rede or the Law of Return. Also, the magic and spells practiced by traditional witches are not necessarily intended to have positive outcomes. If they feel that it is necessary, they may sometimes use hexes and curses against other people without a specific rule that prevents them from doing so.

Belief in witchcraft is widespread throughout Africa, and it is typically blamed for all of the misfortunes that people suffer. In many African countries witchcraft practices are banned, and people suspected of being witches can be severely punished. Some areas even have special witchcraft police, whose job is to hunt for suspected witches and bring them to justice. In M'baiki, a large town in southwestern Africa, several women accused of witchcraft were buried alive in 2002. Other suspected witches have been executed in different ways or have had their houses burned down. But even the threat of punishment and death has not stopped people in Africa from practicing witchcraft because it has been a way of life for too long. Rosemary Ellen Guiley writes, "Ancient tribal customs die hard; modern Africans who wear Western clothing and drive big cars still ask the local witch doctor to bless their homes and petition the gods for safety."[59] People of the Azande tribe in north-central Africa refer to witchcraft as *mangu*, and they believe it is a hereditary skill that is passed from parent to child. They also believe that people who possess *mangu* are not necessarily aware of it. Nightmares are considered to be witch attacks, and it is believed that a witch's spirit can escape during the night and attack the spirit of a victim while the unsuspecting witch is fast asleep.

A type of witchcraft known as hoodoo also has roots in ancient Africa and was brought to America by African slaves. Hoodoo is often confused with the religion of voodoo (also called vodoun),

Did You Know?

Because they practice similar rituals, traditional witches are often confused with Wiccans. Traditional witches believe in the existence of deities, but unlike the Wiccans, they do not regard gods and goddesses as supreme beings.

which is practiced in West Africa and in Haiti. Hoodoo, however, is different because it is not a religion. It incorporates teachings from a number of spiritual movements, and it emphasizes a person's own individual mystical and magical powers.

People who practice hoodoo believe they can access supernatural forces within themselves to improve their lives. They use powers such as divination and necromancy (conjuring the dead to communicate with their spirits), and they perform magic rituals with roots, herbs, bodily fluids, and sometimes body parts from dead animals. A woman from California named Catherine "Cat" Yronwode is well known for her hoodoo skills. She has a shop in Forestville, California, called the Lucky Mojo Curio Company, which carries a variety of spiritual supplies such as herbs, occult oils, incense, and candles. In addition, it also sells what Yronwode refers to as "spell kits for those who cast magic spells, love spells, money spells, and protection spells in the African-American hoodoo, Pagan magick, and other Witchcraft traditions."[60] Yronwode also has her own radio show, called the Lucky Mojo Hoodoo Rootwork Hour, and she teaches an online class in hoodoo that is entitled "Hoodoo Herb and Root Magic."

Did You Know?

Some types of witches believe that the seventh son of a seventh son possesses unusually special powers.

A type of witchcraft that is similar to hoodoo is known as powwowing. It is practiced by Pennsylvania Dutch Christians who believe they are blessed with supernatural powers. Powwowing focuses on healing illness, protecting livestock, putting hexes on enemies, removing hexes that have already been cast by other witches, and driving out evil spirits. The most skilled powwow practitioners are thought to be hereditary witches who were born with skills such as clairvoyance (seeing things outside the normal senses), precognition (seeing into the future), and the ability to heal people by laying their hands on them.

Guiley writes, "Powwowers also offer charms for protecting the household, livestock and crops from misfortune, witchcraft and evil spirits, and for success in virtually every kind of endeavor, from hunting to games to lawsuits to love."[61] Witches who use powwowing may be either women or men, although according to powwowing tradition, the seventh son of a seventh son is believed to possess unusually special powers.

Magic and Spells

Despite the type of witchcraft they practice, witches share a belief in the power and beauty of magic. Wiccans and traditional witches take their magic so seriously that they spell it *magick* to differentiate it from the magic entertainment that is performed by stage magicians. "Magick is beautiful," writes Gwinevere Rain. "We need to embrace its power and majesty, not shove it in the corner where dust gathers! Magick is a part of us, a part of this path, to be respected and used whenever your inner compass suggests."[62]

Witches typically believe that magic comes from the vast power of nature: earth, air, fire, and water. When they perform magic, they feel that they are tapping into this power by having the energy flow into their bodies. Wiccan witches believe that magic results from their becoming one with gods and goddesses during rituals, which puts them in tune with the immense energy possessed by the deities. Once witches are in possession of the energy, they can direct it to effect positive changes in themselves, their environment, and their lives. Author Denise Zimmermann shares her views about this: "Magic itself is not black or white—it's just energy. It's the people who use it who decide whether to use it for good or for negative purposes. You've got

Witches believe that magic comes from the vast power of nature: earth, fire, water, and air. When they perform magic, they feel that they are tapping into this power by having the energy flow into their bodies.

good people and bad people in any religion. There is good and bad in the world, and the whole lesson in life is to keep everything in balance. That's what we try to do."[63] Wiccan witches do not believe in using hexes, curses, or other types of black magic in order to cause harm, which differentiates their type of witchcraft from that of many other witches. One exception was Sybil Leek, a world-famous British Wiccan witch who believed that curses were acceptable if used against one's enemies.

Depending on what kind of witchcraft they practice, many witches often perform a ritual known as "casting a circle" before using their magic or performing spells. This is thought to create a sacred and purified space in which magic work and ceremonies can be performed while keeping unfriendly spirits and negative thoughts out. Rain says that the sacred circle offers witches a place where they can open their minds and reach higher levels of consciousness, as she explains: "It also helps to achieve the desired ritual frame of mind—calm, receptive, intuitive, yet focused. The circle is created from the practitioner's personal energy, blessing of divinity, power of the four elements, as well as a physically defined and visualized psychic barrier."[64]

Many witches perform their magic in front of an altar, which Wiccan witches consider to be their holy place, a place of comfort and power, and a personal expression of their spirituality and their faith. Rain writes, "The altar is to Wiccans what a church is for Christians. It is a place where prayers are heard, messages are sent, tears of both sadness and joy spring free. The altar is more than a simple table or shelf, it is a creation that directly links practitioners to the divine."[65]

Witches accomplish their acts of magic by casting spells, either while they are together with other witches of their covens or when they are alone. They carefully choose the right time to cast spells, such as during a full moon, when the greatest amount of magical power is possible. Witches believe that spells are magical formulas that can change or influence people or events. The spells can be cast in a variety of ways, such as through quiet meditation, chanting, reciting incantations, singing, or while performing certain rituals. Witches use spells for such purposes as protection from disaster, good health, controlling the weather, fertility, career success, wealth, or love, and some witches use spells to punish their adversaries or bring harm to their enemies.

In order to cast a successful spell, they may go into trance-like states so they can devote their concentration to the goal they want to accomplish. According to Buckland, an essential part of spell casting is the witch's belief that the spell really is going to bring about the desired result. He explains:

> You must want whatever you are working at to really happen. You must want it with all of your being. You must put every infinite particle of power into that desire, that urge for the act to come to pass. For this reason, it is usually far more effective to do magick for yourself than to do it on someone else's behalf. It is seldom that another person can feel as intensely about something as the one directly concerned. This strong "feeling" is, in effect, the raised "power" used in magick.[66]

Witches carefully choose the right time to cast spells, such as during a full moon, when the greatest amount of magical power is possible. Witches claim much of their power comes from the moon.

Graham Wyley tells of a simple spell that can be used for house cleansing, or ridding a home of negative energy that may be lingering from the past. The spell consists of visiting every room in the house and opening all doors, cupboards, and closets. "Then," he writes, "with a calm, comforting, sincere and positive mental approach, demand the dismissal of any negative energy by emitting your own loving personality and gratitude towards a happy liaison with the occupiers and the property."[67] In *Confessions of a Teenage Witch,* Rain offers spells for putting an end to gossip, healing, prosperity, more-effective studying, protection, inner peace, an invitation for love, nixing bullies, finding a job, and achieving restful sleep.

Gazing into the Future

Along with magic and spell casting, many witches practice the skill of divination to find the answers to questions about the past, present, and future. Divination is often called fortune-telling, but that is not completely correct. Rain explains that its true goal is to "learn possible outcomes and reveal hidden choices. It is a process of being receptive to the energies within and using them to take a step in the right direction."[68] One method of divination is known as *scrying,* an ancient art in which clairvoyance is achieved by concentrating upon an object with a shiny surface. A popular *scrying* tool is the crystal ball, although witches may also use polished stones, darkened mirrors, or bowls of water. They stare at the shiny, reflective surface until the energy around them causes visions to appear. For some witches the images have appeared right away, but others say they first see a cloud of fog or mist and then gradually the images begin to form.

In some parts of the world, divination is achieved through the use of necromancy, which involves using rituals to conjure the spirits of the dead. Because the spirits no longer have physical bodies and are not bound by earthly restrictions, it is thought that they have access to information beyond that which is available to the living. Necromancy rituals often take place late at night in a graveyard, where witches try to summon ghostly spirits to appear. In voodoo necromancy rituals, appeals are first made to

Baron Samedi, the god of graveyards and zombies. The grave of a corpse is selected (preferably that of someone who is recently deceased), and white candles are placed at the foot of the grave, along with a coat and silk top hat to symbolize the baron's clothing. After the candles are lit, a ritual is performed to awaken the god from his sleep. The witches pay homage to him and promise him offerings of food, drink, and money and then put him back to sleep by tossing roots and herbs onto the ground. Then they unearth the chosen corpse and a designated witch begins asking it questions and receiving answers from its spirit. Following the ritual, the necromancers often burn the corpse or rebury it so it will not be disturbed again.

Although Wiccan witches do not practice necromancy, many

Pictured are Tarot cards and other tools that some witches use to help them see into the future. Although commonly known as fortune-telling, witches believe the true goal is to learn possible outcomes and reveal hidden choices for people.

do communicate with spirits of the dead. This is most common during the sabbat of Samhain, which is when Wiccans believe the veil between the living world and the other-world is at its thinnest. During Samhain, the dead are thought to be able to communicate with the living more easily than at any other time of the year. As Guiley explains, "The souls of the dead come into the land of the living."[69]

One method of divination, or peering into the future, is achieved by concentrating upon an object with a shiny surface such as a crystal ball. Witches stare at the shiny, reflective surface until the energy around them causes visions to appear.

A Witch's Tools

Witches possess a variety of tools that they either purchase or make by hand. One of the most important tools is a knife known as the *athame*. This knife typically has a long black handle and a double-edged steel blade, and witches often customize it by carving it with magical symbols indicative of deities, spirits, or the elements of nature. The *athame* is considered a tool of command and is used to direct energy that is passed from the gods and goddesses to the witch. It is used in the ritual of circle casting; to consecrate, or make sacred, other tools; to channel personal power; and to banish negative energies.

Before the *athame* is used, it must be carefully cleansed of all negative energies and then consecrated by exposing it to all four elements. It is immersed or sprinkled with holy water, touches a flame, passes through the smoke of burning incense, and then either touches a piece of earth or plunges into the ground so it can be charged with Earth's energy. Wyley explains another possible step in the process: "Should it be a clear, starry night when this ceremony is being performed then tools are laid on a windowsill

A Very Visible Witch

Many witches blend in with the crowd because they look and act just like everyone else when they are in public. But that is not the case with Laurie Cabot. Known as "the Official Witch of Salem," Cabot is a Wiccan high priestess who is very visible, with long gray hair that tumbles over her shoulders and back and heavy black makeup on her eyes. She dresses in silky, flowing black gowns, wears a large gold pentacle on a chain around her neck, and covers

so they can be bathed in the rays of the silvery moon. The moon is the source of the witch's power, drawn down from the sky; it is the worker of Magic."[70] Once the *athame* has been cleansed and consecrated, it is to be used only by the witch to whom it belongs and never to be used for any other purpose than witchcraft.

One of the most magical witch tools is the wand, which represents the life force of a witch and symbolizes power, wisdom, and healing. Wands are used to direct magical energy during spell casting, to evoke the power of the deities, to bestow blessings, her fingers in gold and silver rings. From a very young age, Cabot was said to possess psychic powers and often got into trouble for discussing things she learned through extrasensory perception. She has long felt a connection to witches and believes she is descended from a long line of them, including a witch who lived as long as 5,000 years ago.

Today Cabot owns and operates a shop in Salem known as The Cat, the Crow, and the Crown, which she refers to as a magical witch's cottage on her Web site. She has been involved in many civil rights movements to help change the images of witches and has written numerous books on the subject of witchcraft.

to charge objects with energy, and to take the place of an *athame* to cast the circle. Traditionally, witch wands are made from the wood of a sacred tree such as a willow, alder, oak, apple, peach, hazel, or cherry, and some wands are tipped with crystals or precious stones to increase their magical powers.

Another tool that is important to witches is the broom. Long associated with mythical witches who ride through the night sky, brooms are revered by modern witches as sacred tools. They are used for different purposes, but their primary purpose is to purify and protect. Before performing magic, witches use brooms to cleanse a circle or other sacred space by symbolically sweeping away negative energies.

Like brooms, black iron pots known as cauldrons have also been associated with fairy-tale witches, but they too are considered important tools to the modern witch. Cauldrons are used for making brews and potions and as vessels where small fires are burned during spell casting. They may also be used for *scrying;* a witch fills the cauldron with water and gazes into its depths to study reflections and foresee the future.

Did You Know?

Witch wands are made from the wood of a sacred tree such as a willow, alder, oak, apple, peach, hazel, or cherry, and some wands are tipped with crystals or precious stones to increase their magical powers.

Is Witchcraft Real?

Although throughout the world thousands of people consider themselves witches and regularly practice magic, there is no scientific proof that witchcraft exists. In the same way that skeptics doubt the existence of psychic powers such as extrasensory perception, they believe that witchcraft is nothing but a hoax. Brian A. Pavlac is one of those skeptics, saying that he considers "that any people who like to think that they are themselves witches are free to do so. But no one has been able to prove that things like magic/magick. . . . have any scientific validity. All such supernatural stuff, from alien visits to earth to the Devil possessing young girls is insufficiently supported by sound facts, both historically and today."[71]

In the absence of scientific proof, witches are often thought to be people with nothing more than vivid imaginations and a curiosity to explore the unknown. But for those who believe in witchcraft, there is no doubt that they are able to tap into the vast powers of energy and perform magic. They are well aware that many people doubt them, and there are still people who scorn them and falsely believe that witchcraft and devil worship are the same thing. Witches who are true to their craft, however, do not let that discourage them from pursuing what they believe in and are passionate about. Throughout the centuries, witchcraft has managed to survive even though much of the world has tried to extinguish it. Leo Ruickbie writes:

> We have come full circle. . . . We have plumbed the depths of human wickedness, not through witchcraft, but against it. We have found that despite centuries of the most brutal repression . . . and most willful distortion, the Pagan ideals of man in harmony and communication with Nature have re-emerged, as indestructible as the sun, to shine out once more in the new religion of Witchcraft. All the considerable powers of the Inquisition and the basest instincts of mankind were insufficient to root out the irrepressible, magical spirit of us all. The Witches ride again, not on broomsticks to some diabolical orgy of evil, but on the wings of the spirit to a better world, a re-enchanted world.[72]

Did You Know?

Throughout the world thousands of people consider themselves witches and regularly practice magic; however there is no scientific proof that witchcraft exists.

NOTES

Introduction: The Great Unknown

1. Leo Ruickbie, *Witchcraft Out of the Shadows: A Complete History.* London: Robert Hale, 2004, pp. 9–10.
2. Graham Wyley, *The Illustrated Guide to Witchcraft.* New York: Gramercy, 1998, p. 8.

Chapter 1: The History of Witchcraft

3. Raymond Buckland, *Buckland's Complete Book of Witchcraft.* St. Paul: Llewellyn, 2002, pp. 1–2.
4. Buckland, *Buckland's Complete Book of Witchcraft,* p. 2.
5. Rosemary Ellen Guiley, *The Encyclopedia of Witches and Witchcraft.* New York: Facts On File, 1989, p. 104.
6. Quoted in Spring Wolf, "Celtic Shamanism," The Pagan's Path. www.paganspath.com.
7. Ruckbie, *Witchcraft Out of the Shadows,* pp. 36–37.
8. Buckland, *Buckland's Complete Book of Witchcraft,* p. 5.
9. Brian A. Pavlac, "Ten Common Errors and Myths About the Witch-Hunts, Corrected and Commented," October 31, 2001. http://departments.kings.edu.
10. Editors of Time-Life Books, *Witches and Witchcraft.* Alexandria, VA: Time-Life, 1990, pp. 53–54.
11. Jenny Gibbons, "A New Look at the Great European Witch-Hunt," Beliefnet, Autumn 1999. www.beliefnet.com.
12. Amy Cowles, "Black Cats, Werewolves, and Witches: Halloween Symbols Unmasked," *Johns Hopkins Gazette,* October 27 2003. www.jhu.edu.
13. Guiley, *The Encyclopedia of Witches and Witchcraft,* p. 170.
14. Quoted in Ruickbie, *Witchcraft Out of the Shadows,* p. 71.
15. Guiley, *The Encyclopedia of Witches and Witchcraft,* p. 222.
16. Ruickbie, *Witchcraft Out of the Shadows,* p. 74.

Chapter 2: Doomed to Die

17. Guiley, *The Encyclopedia of Witches and Witchcraft,* p. 383.
18. Quoted in Guiley, *The Encyclopedia of Witches and Witchcraft,* p. 342.
19. Guiley, *The Encyclopedia of Witches and Witchcraft,* p. 343.
20. Quoted in Sandra Miesel, "Who Burned the Witches?" *Crisis,* October 2001. www.crisismagazine.com.
21. Wyley, *The Illustrated Guide to Witchcraft,* p. 105.
22. Ruickbie, *Witchcraft Out of the Shadows,* p. 76.
23. Quoted in Hanover Historical Texts Project, "The Witch Persecution at Bamberg." http://history.hanover.edu.
24. Quoted in Guiley, *The Encyclopedia of Witches and Witchcraft,* p. 177.
25. Wyley, *The Illustrated Guide to Witchcraft,* p. 97.
26. Wyley, *The Illustrated Guide to Witchcraft,* p. 98.
27. Wyley, *The Illustrated Guide to Witchcraft,* pp. 98–99.
28. Ruickbie, *Witchcraft Out of the Shadows,* pp. 78–79.

Chapter 3: Witch Hysteria in the New World

29. Quoted in Marc Aronson, *Witch-Hunt: Myster-*

ies of the Salem Witch Trials. New York: Atheneum, 2003, p. 23.

30. Quoted in Goody Glovers.com, "Goodwife 'Goody' Ann Glover." www.goodyglovers.com.
31. Quoted in Aronson, *Witch-Hunt*, p. 60.
32. Aronson, *Witch-Hunt*, p. 73.
33. Quoted in Aronson, *Witch-Hunt*, p. 67.
34. Guiley, *The Encyclopedia of Witches and Witchcraft*, p. 293.
35. Quoted in Aronson, *Witch-Hunt*, p. 106.
36. Aronson, *Witch-Hunt*, p. 113.
37. Quoted in Aronson, *Witch-Hunt*, p. 131.
38. Quoted in Salem, Massachusetts: The City Guide, "The Salem Witch Trials, 1692: A Chronology of Events." www.salemweb.com.
39. Guiley, *The Encyclopedia of Witches and Witchcraft*, p. 297.
40. Aronson, *Witch-Hunt*, p. 5.
41. Quoted in Aronson, *Witch-Hunt*, p. 181.
42. Quoted in Guiley, *The Encyclopedia of Witches and Witchcraft*, p. 300.

Chapter 4: "An' It Harm None"

43. Gwinevere Rain, *Confessions of a Teenage Witch.* New York: Berkley, 2005, p. 4.
44. Kaatryn MacMorgan, "What Is Wicca, Anyway?" Church of Universal Eclectic Wicca, 2003. www.cuew.org.
45. Quoted in Buckland, *Buckland's Complete Book of Witchcraft*, p. 10.
46. Buckland, *Buckland's Complete Book of Witchcraft*, p. 10.
47. Quoted in Editors of Time-Life Books, *Witches and Witchcraft*, p. 115.
48. Catherine Noble Beyer, "Defining Wicca," Wicca: For the Rest of Us, 2005. http://web.archive.org.
49. Rain, *Confessions of a Teenage Witch*, p. 26.
50. MacMorgan, "What Is Wicca, Anyway?"
51. Rain, *Confessions of a Teenage Witch*, p. 42.
52. Catherine Noble Beyer, "The God and Goddess," Wicca: For the Rest of Us. http://web.archive.org.
53. Guiley, *The Encyclopedia of Witches and Witchcraft*, p. 377.
54. The Church of Universal Eclectic Wicca, Homepage. www.cuew.org.
55. Rain, *Confessions of a Teenage Witch*, p. 3.
56. Guiley, *The Encyclopedia of Witches and Witchcraft*, p. 289.
57. Quoted in ReligiousTolerance.org, "Wicca: A Neopagan, Earth-Centered Religion." www.religioustolerance.org.

Chapter 5: Modern Witchcraft

58. Buckland, *Buckland's Complete Book of Witchcraft*, p. xiii.
59. Guiley, *The Encyclopedia of Witches and Witchcraft*, p. 3.
60. Lucky Mojo Curio Company, Homepage. www.luckymojo.com
61. Guiley, *The Encyclopedia of Witches and Witchcraft*, p. 274.
62. Rain, *Confessions of a Teenage Witch*, p. 31.
63. Quoted in Brian Handwerk, "Halloween Shines Light on Witchcraft Today," *National Geographic News*, October 28, 2002. http://news.nationalgeographic.com.
64. Rain, *Confessions of a Teenage Witch*, p. 109.
65. Rain, *Confessions of a Teenage Witch*, p. 59.
66. Buckland, *Buckland's Complete Book of Witchcraft*, p. 35.
67. Wyley, *The Illustrated Guide to Witchcraft*, p. 78.
68. Rain, *Confessions of a Teenage Witch*, p. 21.
69. Guiley, *The Encyclopedia of Witches and Witchcraft*, p. 289.
70. Wyley, *The Illustrated Guide to Witchcraft*, p. 61.
71. Pavlac, "Ten Common Errors and Myths About the Witch-Hunts, Corrected and Commented."
72. Ruickbie, *Witchcraft Out of the Shadows*, p. 223.

GLOSSARY

clairvoyance: Seeing things outside the normal senses.

consecrate: To make sacred.

coven: An organized group of witches.

deity: A supernatural being, such as a god or goddess.

divination: The magical art of unlocking the secrets of the unknown.

druid: An ancient Celtic priest.

heresy: The act of speaking out against Christianity's official teachings.

hoodoo: A form of witchcraft that originated in Africa.

monotheistic: The belief that there is only one God.

pagan: A person with beliefs that are centered on the earth and nature.

sabbat: One of eight holidays celebrated by Wiccans.

shaman: A spiritual person who uses supernatural powers to heal.

specter: An apparition, or something that exists only in appearance.

tradition: A denomination or branch of Wicca.

Wicca: An earth-based religion that is centered in nature and the seasons.

Wiccan Rede: A guiding moral principle for people of the Wiccan religion.

witch's mark: A small blemish, birthmark, or even invisible spot that was thought to be the mark of the devil on a witch.

For Further Research

Books

Ellen Dugan, *Elements of Witchcraft: Natural Magick for Teens.* St. Paul: Llewellyn, 2003. The author, who has practiced witchcraft for more than 15 years, provides information about her craft, including the importance of harnessing personal power by making use of Earth's natural forces.

Rosemary Ellen Guiley, *The Encyclopedia of Witches and Witchcraft.* New York: Facts On File, 1999. An excellent, comprehensive book that answers most any question related to witches throughout history.

Lauren Manoy, *Where to Park Your Broomstick: A Teen's Guide to Witchcraft.* New York: Fireside, 2002. This book covers the history of paganism and witchcraft, witchcraft in modern times, and spells, recipes, and advice from teen witches.

Gwinevere Rain, *Confessions of a Teenage Witch.* New York: Penguin Putnam, 2005. A complete guide to Wicca as told from the perspective of a young author who has been a practicing Wiccan since she was 14 years old.

Lisa Yount, *At Issue in History: The Salem Witch Trials.* San Diego: Greenhaven, 2002. A book about the people who were accused of being witches and were executed in Salem during the late seventeenth century.

Denise Zimmermann and Katherine Gleason, *Complete Idiot's Guide to Wicca and Witchcraft.* Indianapolis: Alpha, 2006. A beginner's guide to the history of Wicca and witchcraft, including the customs and practices used by today's Wiccans.

Periodicals

Marcel Bucher, "Bewitched Switzerland," *Swiss News,* December 2004.

Stephen Jo Grant, "Wiccan Holidays," *Skipping Stones,* November/December 2004.

Simon de Trey-White, "The Witches of Gambaga," *Geographical,* August 2006.

Internet Source

Amy Cowles, "Black Cats, Werewolves, and Witches: Halloween Symbols Unmasked," *Johns Hopkins University Gazette,* October 27, 2003. www.jhu.edu/~gazette/2003/27oct03/27symbol.html.

Web Sites

How Stuff Works: How Witchcraft Works (http://science.howstuffworks.com/witchcraft.htm). This Web site discusses the different types of witchcraft, witch hunts throughout history, and Wicca. It also includes links to other witch-related sources.

Religious Tolerance: Wicca (www.religioustolerance.org/witchcra.htm). This site boasts a large collection of information, including the history of Wicca, frequently asked questions about Wicca, myths and facts about witch persecution, a timeline of the witch hunts in Europe, and a section called "Teens and Wicca."

Salem, Massachusetts: The City Guide (www.salemweb.com/guide/witches.shtml). The online article "What About Witches" includes interesting information about the Salem witch trials.

Teen Witch (www.teenwitch.com). A site designed especially for teenagers who are interested in learning more about the Wiccan religion and witchcraft.

Index

E

F

G

H

I

About the Author

Peggy J. Parks holds a bachelor of science degree from Aquinas College in Grand Rapids, Michigan, where she graduated magna cum laude. She is a freelance author who has written more than 60 nonfiction books for children and young adults. Parks lives in Muskegon, Michigan, a town that she says inspires her writing because of its location on the shores of Lake Michigan.